Lead Yourself First!

The Senior Leader's Guide to Engaging Your People for Greater Performance and Impact

by

Dr. Karen Y. Wilson-Starks

**Lead Yourself First!
The Senior Leader's Guide to Engaging Your People for Greater Performance and Impact**
by Dr. Karen Y. Wilson-Starks

Copyright © 2018 Dr. Karen Y. Wilson Starks
Published by SkillBites LLC
www.skillbites.net

All rights reserved.
No part of this book may be reproduced or transmitted in any form or by any means whatsoever without written permission from the author, except in the case of brief quotations embodied in critical articles and reviews.

DISCLAIMER AND/OR LEGAL NOTICES

While the publisher and authors have used their best efforts in preparing this book, they make no representations or warranties with respect to the accuracy or completeness of the contents of this book. The advice and strategies contained herein may not be suitable for your situation. You should consult a professional where appropriate. Neither the publisher nor the authors shall be liable for any loss of profit or any other commercial damages, including but not limited to special, incidental, consequential, or other damages. The purchaser or reader of this publication assumes responsibility for the use of these materials and information. Adherence to all applicable laws and regulations, both advertising and all other aspects of doing business in the United States or any other jurisdiction, is the sole responsibility of the purchaser or reader.

ISBN-10: 1-942489-64-1

ISBN-13: 978-1-942489-64-1

Dedication

In memory of my mother, Yvonne B. Wilson, my first role model of the entrepreneurial spirit; my maternal grandmother, Carrin M. Bowens, for modeling friendship and hospitality; and my paternal grandmother, Rosa Wilson, for demonstrating perseverance and faith under daunting circumstances.

In honor of my husband, Gregory Starks, for his ongoing love and support and my father, Morris L. Wilson Sr., for always encouraging and believing in me and my dreams.

This book is dedicated to Erica Y. Redmond, Keiyehn Gray, Keimora Gray, and all of my other nieces, nephews, great-nieces, great-nephews, and godchildren as they continue to build success in their lives and careers. My heart's desire is that they will be inspired to use their gifts and talents to serve others and make a lasting impact on the world and next generations as they live out their unique callings.

Acknowledgments

No writing project comes to completion without a lifetime of deposits from those closest to us. I thank my husband, Gregory Starks, for encouraging the vision of this book and for reading an early manuscript. Your love and encouragement have been like the water of life to help me grow and blossom on my journey. I thank my sister, Valerie J. Kimble, for her love, encouragement, support, and early manuscript reading. Valerie, words can't describe how much I have valued and benefited from your input. Thanks to my father, Morris L. Wilson Sr., for laying and helping me to grow a foundation of spiritual connection with God, my brothers, Morris L. Wilson Jr. and Jeffrey M. Wilson, for answering every call to support all my endeavors, and to other relatives who have loved, encouraged, and challenged me on my journey—Anita L. Wilson (step-mother), Hattie Starks (mother-in-law), Angela Williams (Great-Aunt Jean), Julia C. Kent (godmother), and so many more too numerous to mention.

A very special thank you goes to all of my clients and colleagues from whom I have learned a lifetime of lessons. It's been my privilege to walk and serve with you, and I look forward to many more productive years together. Without my experiences with you there would be no book. I also deeply thank my long-term business mentor Dr. Alan Weiss for giving me the knowledge and tools to build a more substantial and significant business. I am grateful for all the lessons I have learned from you and thank you so much for sharing them with me.

Thanks to my publisher, Judy Weintraub of SkillBites, who was gracious enough to accept this project despite my hectic schedule and tight deadlines. Thanks also to my editors at The Red to Black Editing Company who greatly improved the readability of this manuscript. Your collective abilities have really made a significant positive difference. I also want to thank Chad Barr, my web designer, and his team at the Chad Barr Group for their creativity, innovation, and multiple ways of showing me how to create a more powerful web presence.

Thanks most of all to God for daily life, wisdom, and direction to fulfill my life's purpose. Neither my work nor this book would be possible without inspiration from the One who daily sustains and fills me.

Table of Contents

Acknowledgments 4

Introduction 1

Chapter One - Envision the Future 7

Chapter Two - Run Your Own Race 21

Chapter Three - Forge Your Own Pathway 33

Chapter Four - Focus on the Positive 45

Chapter Five - Build Strength, Fortitude, and Confidence through Challenges 53

Chapter Six - Learn from Others 61

Chapter Seven - Feed Your Spirit 69

Chapter Eight - Practice Gratitude 81

Chapter Nine - Encourage and Build Others 87

Chapter Ten - Play Your Music 93

Summary of Lessons Learned 98

Summary of Questions to Ask Yourself 100

Epilogue - Where I Am From 103

Introduction

"To Do Your Best, You Must First Be Your Best"

Sitting in front of me for our first meeting was a handsome man in his early fifties. Successful in past management roles, he had just been promoted to a significant leadership position in his organization. The role he now filled came with a laundry list of longstanding problems. I had a large file of assessment data in front of me detailing my client's personality, leadership style, and effectiveness ratings from his boss, peers, direct reports, and clients. Like many executives, he focused on his weaknesses, starting to wonder if he was the right man for the job.

"Maybe this was a mistake. Maybe I am not the one and I don't have what it takes. Perhaps someone else should have been selected. What do you think?" he asked.

As I quickly paged through the test results and the biographical information, rereading my notes and highlights, I looked up and said, "I see a man who is visionary, intelligent, and insightful. I see someone who cares deeply about the success of others and this organization. I also see an organization with people who historically have not had the benefit of a visionary leader. In addition, they have not been nurtured or cared for to rise to their greatest potential. They have been managed more than led."

"Do you think I have what it takes?" he asked.

"You have exactly what they need and exactly what it takes. The job is yours if you want it."

"The job is mine if I want it?"

"Yes, you have all the requisite abilities. Yes, you will have to grow, learn new skills and abilities, and yes, there is a steep learning curve; however, you already have the foundation. Are you up for the challenge?"

Introduction

After a few seconds of thought, he said, "Yes, I am ready."

We shook hands and thus began a fruitful client/advisor relationship that led to him successfully turning his organization around to make it one of the most desirable places to work. Instead of employees trying to get out of his organization, people started applying to join the work. In addition, existing employees said, for the first time in a while, that they felt proud to be on the team. Years later, we looked back at that beginning, and he told me that if I had said he didn't have what it took, he would have gone back to the office and resigned. What a tremendous loss for both him and his organization, had that happened.

In my work as an executive leadership development consultant, I call out the greatness in the people and organizations with whom I work. It's from these seeds of greatness that leadership is inspired, nurtured, and grown to larger levels. Without calling out this greatness, leaders and organizations fail to fully transform. It takes tremendous personal growth to lead at the level of significant achievement and impact. You must know and be able to use your signature strengths, gifts, and talents to deploy them most effectively. Much of this knowledge is forged in the fires of life experience and the powerful lessons learned along the way.

As a trusted advisor to corporate, government, military, and nonprofit leaders, I hear my clients' fears, concerns, and worries. Left unchecked, these paralyzing fears keep them from moving forward with ease and confidence. Leadership is about allowing your commitment, dedication, faith, and strength to win out over your fear. It's taking that next step even if that step is all you can see. Vision comes to those who use the vision they have already received.

I am frequently asked by senior leaders to come in and work with their direct reports or with the upper middle managers. If, during such work, the key leader is not part of the experience or an equivalent experience, then the organization grows beyond the key leader's own level of transformation. The direct report and upper middle management leaders who have participated in the development experience now metaphorically speak fluent French while their top leader either doesn't or speaks it on an elementary level.

There is now a communication gap inhibiting the developed upper middle managers from easily using their newfound abilities throughout the organization. These limitations exist because their boss didn't choose to also learn French. Sometimes, the senior leader recognizes she is in Paris speaking English to those who speak French. In the face of blank stares, she steps up and learns to speak French. In other situations, the top leaders limit the organization because they are unable to recognize, understand, and reward this new level of fluency in their people. You must be the leader for the transformed organization you see. Why not start with you?

In this book, I share my own life journey and the lessons I have learned along the way while extracting the principles relevant to other leaders who want to make a significant impact in their sphere of influence. As a trusted advisor, I too have had to follow my own advice to become a vessel of greater capacity. This book is about the self-development ingredients for the senior leader. These ingredients include envisioning the future, running your own race, forging your own pathway, focusing on the positive, building confidence through challenges, learning from others, feeding your spirit, expressing thankfulness and gratitude, encouraging and building others, and ultimately playing the music only you are gifted enough to play.

As the senior leader of your organization, your primary job is to be a leader who is worthy of the organization you want to build. Before you "do" anything, it's necessary to be a person with the wisdom, character, intestinal fortitude, and compassion to lead well. Task-oriented, bottom-line-driven, practical leaders often want to start with the "how-to"; however, it's difficult to pour a gallon of water into a pint-sized glass. First get

Introduction

a bigger container and then you will be able to retain and drink all the water you want.

If you are committed to both being and doing the best for your organization, then this book is for you. You know that you are building something great. Your challenge is to move yourself and your organization from one level of greatness to the next. You know that to *do* your best, you must first *be* your best. You want to learn, grow, and expand your capacity to use and benefit from tactical how-to information already available elsewhere. This book is more about the strategic part of engaging your people for greater performance and impact.

Lead Yourself First! You are the instrument of your leadership. Tune up and get ready to play your music—the journey starts with you. Meet me in Chapter One to continue our journey together.

Chapter One

Envision the Future

"Doors Open When We Envision a Compelling Future"

Roadblocks on the Path to Success

From an early age, I was one of those children who valued learning and education. Although it wasn't an assignment, I read all the books in my first grade's in-class library and was fascinated by all the new worlds available to visit through the written word. In those early years, I imagined that one day I'd be a teacher.

Later, when I was in the third grade, immediately after Christmas, my family moved from our neighborhood to a much nicer one. The houses in the new neighborhood were beautiful custom homes from an earlier generation. They were large, well-made, detached buildings with history and character. The tree-lined streets were peaceful and gorgeous. My previous neighborhood consisted of row houses—customary for Baltimore—and there weren't many trees. The new neighborhood, filled with enterprising middle class Black residents, had previously been inhabited by Jewish people and was well-maintained. All the doorposts in the house still had mezuzahs attached.

Since our new neighborhood was a significant upgrade, I assumed that the school would also be better. Although my previous school consisted of all Black children, our principal was a Caucasian man with a PhD. For a working-class Black neighborhood, we had valuable resources and age-appropriate learning materials.

As soon as my father walked me into the new school, I knew that I didn't belong. The school was very old and physically ugly, reminiscent of a prison. That alone probably would not have deterred me; however, the children were wild, undisciplined, and in all ways unruly. I was shocked upon seeing this scene and started crying. I told my father, "Daddy, don't leave me here." I don't know if he saw what I saw, though it was clear that I had to go to school and would not be allowed to return home. Thus began the worst half-year in my whole academic history.

Every book that we had in the third grade was a book I had read one or two years prior. Not being one to repeat the same lessons, I asked for new books, yet every time they found me one, I had already read it in my previous school. The books we received were hand-me-downs from other schools. They were used and in poor condition. At my previous school, the books were new and exciting and not previously possessed by other students.

During that half-year, I had at least five different teachers and I didn't learn much. The one thing I really remember was our weekly square-dancing lesson. There was one Caucasian boy in our school who happened to be in my class and who liked having me as a square dance partner. Although they didn't teach math, reading, or science, they were very deliberate about teaching square dancing. To this day, I hate square dancing because I associate it with the conspiracy to keep me uneducated.

Sometimes the present will not look anything like the future you envision. You may even wonder if you can get there from where you are now. The key to success is recognizing that the future vision is more powerful than any present roadblock. The roadblock is only temporary so long as you recognize you will find ways to go over, under, and around the roadblock, or even remove it. The point is, even the roadblock can become an instrument to help you reach your destination—if you have a destination.

You are building leadership muscle when you learn to hurdle that roadblock and keep your vision clearly in view. Leadership is about overcoming obstacles; you can't really say you are a leader if you haven't had to deal with any serious challenges since it's easy to lead in good times. Leaders don't stop when they hit a roadblock; they remember they have someplace to go beyond that roadblock. These are times to develop your determination and best strategic thinking. In my case, I had to forge a pathway forward in spite of square dancing and the "prison" school.

Hope on the Horizon

One day an announcement came out that we were to take home to our parents. There was an opportunity to go to a public school in a Jewish neighborhood—what we would ultimately refer to as the "Jewish school." I saw this opportunity as my ticket out of the prison of this intellectually impoverished lifestyle.

I presented the announcement to my parents and said, "This is what I want to do. Send me to the Jewish school." As far as I was concerned, there was nothing to think about.

My parents were worried and said, "If you go to this school you will have to take a school bus and it's a long way." I already walked two miles to my current school and the bus would leave from there.

I didn't care what sacrifices were required—I just knew that to realize my vision, I had to get out of where I was. Maybe a little melodramatic, yet I felt that my life was wasting away and that spending any more time in this school would cause me to hate school and education. As an eager learner, I had never hated either.

My parents went to the school and had a conference with my teacher. As the oldest of four children, I had one younger brother in school with me while our two younger siblings were not yet school age.

The teacher told my parents, "Your child does not belong in this school. We recommend that she have the opportunity to go to the Jewish School."

My parents said, "We don't want her to go alone, so we will only agree if her brother can also go."

When the school reviewed my brother's record, they said, "both of your children have excellent academic and conduct records so they both can go." I was relieved.

The next school term, my brother and I started riding the school bus from our previous school and attended the Jewish school through sixth grade. The first day of school, based on my prior academic record, I was placed in the highest reading group. The book may as well have been written in hieroglyphics—I could not understand it. I was then moved to the lowest reading group. The same thing happened in math. I had not learned multiplication in third grade, and now we were learning division. I had to learn both at the same time. I knew I'd have to work hard to catch up with my peers, and I was highly motivated.

By the end of fourth grade, I had caught up with my peers and even had time to run for a political office, though I lost the election to a popular girl in my class. By the time I got to fifth grade, I was doing well academically and I won an election to Parliamentarian of the Student Council. I was so thankful to be at this school where I could learn again. Each classroom had one to three Black students, and except for one Caucasian, non-Jewish boy who was in my class, all of the other Caucasian students were Jewish. Despite the Jewish parents occasionally picketing against us being there, I was determined to learn and succeed.

As a leader, there will be times when your learning curve is steep. Getting to that next level or step on your journey may mean starting at the bottom. You may start, metaphorically, in the lowest reading group; however, you are going to surpass this reading group even though you start there. A true leader has the humility to acknowledge what they don't yet know and to take the steps to learn the necessary lessons.

As one on a leadership mission, be thankful for new growth opportunities. Your boss wants to promote you and you know it will mean getting out of your comfort zone, leaving the place of ease and entering a new area where you are not yet the expert.

Many have stifled their careers because they didn't want to feel that temporary dip in performance as they moved forward.

One of my clients was in a comfortable job in a prestigious company, the kind of organization you want to have listed on your resume. She was well compensated, respected, and had access to needed resources. She knew she had learned all she could learn from her job and organization; to really grow and fulfill her life purpose she needed to leave and start her own business. Leaving was not easy since so many people, including her boss, had made significant deposits into her leadership growth. We crafted an exit plan that allowed her to honor those who had been integral to her journey, to leave at the right time, and to create her landing pad for the new company. She left on her terms with great relationships intact and a bright future with new clients already on board for her new venture.

You may have to go to a new position, a new company, or a new country to take your next step. Be willing to stretch, grow, learn, and become the best. Challenge yourself by associating with others who are ahead of you. Be willing to sharpen your saw so that you as an instrument can work with greater precision.

Proclaiming the Vision

In the sixth grade, I decided to become a psychologist. I didn't know much about the field, yet I imagined it to be like what Dear Abby provided in the way of advice and counsel in the local newspaper. I was both a "psychologist" and "consultant" from a young age. I helped my brothers and sister and neighborhood children with issues and even started a little newspaper called *Dear Nerak* (Karen spelled backwards). Even my parents sought my counsel on various issues, and hence was born my consulting career.

Both of my parents were high school graduates; it wasn't until later in life that my mother became a nurse and my father got a bachelor's degree in urban planning. The only thing I knew about being a psychologist was that I'd have to go to college. At that time, I didn't know that a doctorate was also required. With each advancing year, I learned of more requirements and just added these to my list of things I'd need to do to reach my objective. I was committed to taking all necessary steps to prepare for my career. I envisioned myself in a private practice.

My mother's only vision for us was that each of her children would finish high school. I was always ambitious, and she said I was the one who told her and my father what I wanted to do and what was next. They never had to push me because I was self-motivated. The vision of my future was always in clear focus.

I wanted to attend George Pepperdine University in California. I held onto this vision through my first year of college at the University of Maryland, College Park. My parents probably thought I'd forget about George Pepperdine, though I never did. I was very disappointed to hear that my only choices were to go to the University of Maryland or Morgan State College. As an adventurer who had been in a very diverse environment since the fourth grade, I chose Maryland to continue my diverse educational experience.

Many years later, after becoming a psychologist, a friend who had graduated from one of the PhD programs at George Pepperdine invited me to take a tour of the campus on one of what was to be my frequent business trips to California. I was ecstatic to finally see my dream school. When I got to Pepperdine, I was shocked to see such a small campus. The ocean views were spectacular, and my friend assured me that the education was also stellar.

After this visit, I understood why I didn't go to George Pepperdine. Although I had wanted to, a higher power (God) knew that I needed a bigger school filled with more options and possibilities. After this visit, I finally realized that God had seen a greater vision for me than I saw for myself at the time. Given my personality, Maryland was probably a better fit. It was nice to finally make peace with this detail that hadn't gone according to my plan. Sometimes the "how" changes while the greater vision stays intact.

After graduating from Maryland, it was time to attend graduate school. I was accepted into four schools and had narrowed it down to New York University (NYU) and the University of Connecticut at Storrs (UCONN). We had lots of relatives living in New York, so we visited the city most years and I had especially fond memories of living there for the summer of 1965 and seeing the World's Fair. Although I was partial to NYU, my advisors at Maryland spoke of why the University of Connecticut might be a better fit for me. Again, they were right. Although I was from a big city, Baltimore was dwarfed by the hustle and bustle of New York. In addition, NYU offered a psychoanalytic program while the University of Connecticut was geared more toward behavioral and social learning theory. The social learning theory perspective was a better fit for me. In addition, Dr. Julian Rotter, a luminary in the field, was the chair of the clinical psychology department at UCONN.

As you start stepping along your path, your vision will become clearer and more defined. As you learn and experience more, you will see new and different possibilities. Although everything you envisioned may not happen as you originally saw it, that's no impediment to success. In fact, some of the paths you didn't plan to take will turn out to be better for you. Be willing to accept and respond to new information and to have the journey directed by the One in the universe who knows and sees more than you.

As you develop greater clarity about your vision, you will see circumstances and people enter your life to ensure that the vision takes place. There is nothing like the momentum of a vision declared for bringing new energy and resources toward making it happen. Set the vision in front of you so that you can take advantage of these natural currents that catch you and take you further than you'd ever go without this extra boost. Be willing to listen to those who support your vision and have your best interest in mind. You won't always follow what they say, yet sometimes, they will lead you to a better path.

Funding the Vision

My parents had been very instrumental in funding my undergraduate education. In addition, I worked fulltime every summer and part-time during the school year. I inherited a strong work ethic from both parents, who had also identified their dream careers and went after them. Facing my first year in graduate school, I didn't know exactly how I was going to finance the journey. Resourced with a total of $30 in all my bank accounts, my mother, a worrier, wondered how I was going to make it. She reminded me that I would be more than eight hours from home and that she and my father would be unable to help me.

One day when I was feeling discouraged, my resident director at Maryland, an African-American graduate student from Connecticut , encouraged me and let me know that God would make a way. Armed with this newfound confidence, I pressed on to the objective.

I had tremendous faith that a door would open and I'd be able to continue my plan to become a psychologist—though I didn't know how. There was not even a way to take public transportation to UCONN at the time. The summer before school started, my grandmother drove me up to visit the school and to meet with Dr. Rotter.

In that meeting, he said, "I see you have a strong academic record, though you will have to work hard here." His comment made me wonder if he really believed that my academic record was so strong.

In addition, I thought, "He has no idea of the vision in my head and the sacrifices I have already made to get here. Does he think I wasn't working before?" Not once did I doubt my own ability to finish the program. I heard that many African-Americans had started the program, though few went past the first year. Each clinical class accepted only 5-7 students out of hundreds of applicants. It was even more competitive than medical school.

Shortly before school began, I received a letter offering me an Institute of Mental Health Fellowship to fund my first year. And so it would be, funding one year at a time and not knowing what I would do after that. This took tremendous faith. Yet I stayed the course because the vision and commitment were so strong.

For my second year of graduate school, I received a teaching assistantship, and that's how that year was funded. When I got to my third year, the university did not offer me any options, so I found a full-time job on campus that I really liked. Later, when I was looking for internship opportunities, I remembered that many nurses and physicians I knew had spoken quite well of Walter Reed Hospital in Washington, DC. In a desire to expose myself to all the conditions and disorders in the Diagnostic and Statistical Manual of Mental Disorders (DSM), I wrote to Walter Reed. I soon learned that enrollment there would require me to join the Army as an officer. This was not in my plan for success, so I decided to abandon that pursuit.

Eventually, the chief psychologist of the Army called because he was trying his best to get psychologists into the Army while Congress still had a door of opportunity open for the Health Professions Scholarship Program. Although I was nearing the end of my education and most people joined this program at the beginning of their graduate education, the opportunity appealed to me because I knew it would allow me to fund my fourth year of school and give me a chance to go to Walter Reed.

The chief psychologist encouraged me to apply because we were immediately up against the deadline, and if I was selected and chose not to be in the Army, I wouldn't have to take the appointment. This seemed fair enough, so I applied to the Health Professions Scholarship Program in Psychology. Except for a grandfather who served in Germany during World War II, I do not come from a military family, so I had to look far and wide to find friends to interview about what it was like to be in the Army.

Later, after I had been accepted into the program, I met with two recruiters. The first was a hard-as-nails senior Army captain who had already done several tours in the Middle East even though this was way before the Iraq-Afghanistan wars and before you routinely heard of our presence in any middle-eastern country. He was a smoking, drinking, cursing kind of guy, and as far as I was concerned, we had nothing in common. He fit all my stereotypes about who was in the Army, and none of those remotely resembled me. Seeing that I wasn't too comfortable or relating well to him, he was shrewd enough to set me up to meet a young lieutenant and family man who worked for him. I visited with the lieutenant and his family at Fort Devens in Massachusetts. I toured the post, his work place, and his home on the post. The lieutenant was a very religious Mormon and very mild-mannered. I was much more like him than the captain, and I said to myself, "If he can be in the Army, then so can I." Ultimately, I accepted the appointment.

As a business leader you may not always have the financial resources to do what you want to do next. Yet, if you are determined, focused, and serious, you will ultimately find a way. Too many abandon their vision due to lack of financial resources. If you keep your vision in front of you despite financial obstacles, you will discover the ingenuity, creativity, and opportunity to fund your vision. There is an answer to all need, and it comes to you when you relentlessly pursue the intention you have set. Again, lack of resources is only temporary; it's not a permanent condition unless you declare it so. Otherwise, you will find a way.

As a senior leader you signal your team with either hope, abundance, and possibility or with fear, hopelessness, and need. When you signal hope and possibility your people will generate ways forward; this momentum will ignite an unstoppable spark of innovation and positive achievements. If you signal fear and hopelessness, people shut down and look for the escape hatch. You set the tone. Your people want to know if you believe you and they can take the hill. When you lead and show the way, they follow and you take the hill together.

Summary Thoughts on Envisioning the Future

My whole life has been characterized by setting a sharp vision and intention for everything I wanted to accomplish, and everything I have set my mind to do both personally and career-wise has occurred. Armed with this background and experience, I encourage my clients to set a greater vision for themselves and their organizations. I am living proof that envisioning a compelling future opens doors. There may be unexpected twists and turns, but they are all an important part of the journey. Fear keeps many from setting a vision for the future, or they may be stuck with a lack of clarity about the "how." It's been my experience that when the vision is clear, the next "how" always comes along. Since I have been through this process so many times myself, I am able to confidently support my clients through their processes as well.

Vision is about seeing what is beyond the current circumstances and deciding to go someplace different, no matter where you are today. I was once working with a client whose organization needed to grow and scale to remain successful. We were preparing to do a high-level hire that would help him with day-to-day operations. Just as we were poised to launch a team of professionals to recruit, select, and integrate the new hire, the business went through a crisis. My client, the president of the company, wasn't sure he could do a turnaround—though if possible, he predicted it would take about three months. Although this crisis seemed bigger than previous crises, I knew that my client had already gone through other tough times. Like me, I also knew he had a strong work ethic and would do whatever it took to turn the business around.

Although my client feared the business might shut down in three months, I spoke life into his situation and said with great confidence that they would not fail. I knew he would figure it out; failure was not on my radar for him or his company. I also said that I would be praying for him. On that note, we parted with the idea of touching base again in three months. A month and a half later, he called to say the turnaround was done. Wow, and in half the time predicted! He also said he felt the prayers and was confident that I was faithful to pray for them. We then were able to continue what we had previously paused.

To be successful, the key leader must be able to envision the future, a desired next point or end, and not be deterred by not knowing the details of how the vision will be realized. Without a picture in mind of your future, you probably won't get there. There will be aimless drifting and wasting of precious time.

Lessons Learned

1. Set a clear, compelling vision and intention for your life.
2. Have faith that somehow, some way, the vision will come to fruition if you continue to pursue it.
3. Knock until the door or another door opens.

Questions to Ask Yourself

1. What is the compelling vision I hold for myself? For my organization? What do I want to see in the future?
2. How can I encourage myself in pursuing this vision even when what I see in the present seems far from that future picture?
3. What qualities/skills do I already have to realize this vision? What else will I need to learn?

Find out where you score on key leadership development metrics. What are your strengths and development needs in leading yourself? Click or go to the link below to find out:

http://transleadership.com/resources/development1-assessment/

**Take the *"Lead Yourself First"* Leadership Assessment:
http://transleadership.com/resources/development1-assessment/**

Chapter Two

Run Your Own Race

"Running Your Own Race Is Also About Knowing What Motivates You"

Know Your Strengths and Development Needs and Plan Accordingly

The Army Physical Training (PT) test was always a challenge for me. The test consisted of push-ups, sit-ups, and a two-mile run, and we had to qualify twice a year. All segments were timed, and we had to meet or exceed their minimum standards. I was fine with the push-ups and sit-ups, but the two-mile run was another story. There was a reason I favored the 100-yard dash in high school. It wasn't so much that I favored running of any type—rather that I could quickly finish the 100-yard dash and be on to something else more interesting. I never would have signed up for long-distance running—in my mind, two miles was long-distance, even if not considered so by others.

A whole group of us began together at the starting line. Everybody was hyped up and wanted to run their fastest and best. I could feel the tension and the adrenaline rush. On your mark, get set, GO! As soon as the word was said, people flew from that start line like a herd of gazelles being chased by a cheetah. Because I was not a very good or strong runner, I had to train myself to ignore all that speed and energy and focus on running my own race. I already knew that if I moved too fast at the start, I'd likely get a cramp in my calf and have problems on the back end. The key to success was to pace myself.

It took a lot of discipline to ignore the temptation to fly out of that starting gate with everyone else. Instead, I let them leave me in the dust and I started my race at a slower tempo with the idea that I would gradually increase speed and get to what I called my "training zone." I stayed in that relatively fast training zone for most of the race and then sped up at the end to get the benefit of that old high school 100-yard dash. By the time I got to the last 100 yards, my muscles were warmed up and ready to go. Using this strategy, I finished within the standards and was home free for the next six months.

Starting the race at a slower pace allowed me to get my body ready for the journey. By the time I reached my training zone, I was moving with ease at a pretty good clip and each increase in speed was easier. Eyes straight ahead, focused on my destination, and paying attention to my breathing, I sailed down the track. Along the way I saw lots of other soldiers, the same ones who flew out of the gate at breakneck speed, stopped along the way with cramps or out of breath. A tortoise at the beginning, I was now passing the hares. Seeing them on the sidelines only served to confirm once again that I was running the race in the way that worked best for me.

To focus on my own race and do the opposite of what others were doing was not easy. I had to see them and not be thrown off by what I saw. I had to remember that there was a good reason for what I was doing and that it did work. I had to focus more on myself than on what others were doing. I kept that in the forefront and them in the periphery. They were running the race that was best for them, but what was best for them was not necessarily best for me.

You also have your own unique pattern of talents and gifts, and in those areas where you are less strong, you may have to operate differently from others just to get to the finish line. Likewise, for your signature strengths, you may be a hare racing past the rest. The bottom line is to know yourself and your abilities as a leader and to operate with that knowledge squarely in focus.

In the Biblical account, David the shepherd boy knew he could kill Goliath because he had previously killed lions and bears in the course of protecting his father's sheep. King Saul, a seasoned warrior, had killed many enemies using his spear and coat of armor. Wanting to help David, Saul gave him his equipment. David quickly realized that though these worked for Saul, this was not how he knew to fight, so he removed Saul's armor in favor of his lighter clothing and equipment. Most soldiers would not have gone to the battlefield so bare as David, nor would they have taken a slingshot to use against the enemy's more sophisticated weaponry, yet David used what worked for him (I Samuel 17:32-40).

In business, you will also make many choices about what is best for you and your company. You will have to modify some strategies you see or hear about to best fit your unique strengths, abilities, and challenges.

One of my clients, a senior leader in the healthcare field, is often sought out by other institutions that want to recruit him to lead their operations. Most of these "opportunities" turn out not to be the right fit for my client. As he peels back the layers of the institutional and leadership culture, he learns that the institution really wants a safe pair of hands to maintain the status quo. My client is a change agent, so these opportunities feel constraining to him. In his case, to best run his own race, he chooses to stay on his current track where he can continue to bring in rewards and victories. Had he not taken the time to know himself, what he likes, and how he works best, he may have been sidetracked into a less fulfilling lane less suited to his unique skills and abilities. Sometimes the grass is not greener on the other side, and a promotion is not a promotion if it doesn't get you where you need to go.

Popular is Not Always Better

Knowing your own race is learned over time and through many experiences. I had done enough PT tests to know what worked for me. In many situations, you will first get it wrong and then make a course correction. I vividly remember one situation where I had to learn the hard way. In the Army, one of the most difficult, challenging, and physically demanding activities is the twelve-mile forced road march with full field gear weighing about eighty pounds. The road march must be completed within three hours and the whole time you are wearing the uniform with combat boots and carrying an eighty-pound duffle bag on your back. At the time I was 5 feet 4 inches tall and weighed about 130 pounds, so this was no easy feat. To make the time commitment, I had to essentially run the entire race. Since you already know that I consider two miles of running long distance, twelve miles was truly a marathon.

I listened to other soldiers who had been through this before, and they all swore by the virtues of Gatorade to get through this grueling challenge. The key was to keep your electrolytes in balance and Gatorade was supposed to help with this objective. Although I had been an avowed water person for most of my life in all previous physical challenges, I had not yet experienced anything like this. On the day of the road march, I had plenty of Gatorade to get me through the three-hour trial.

The road march is difficult and challenging no matter the circumstances. About three-fourths of the way into the race, I knew I was in trouble. I found that I had tired of the taste of Gatorade and something about it was not agreeing with my body. It was now too late, I couldn't drink enough water to make up for the deficit. Within a hundred yards from the finish line with lots of people cheering on the sidelines, my body could not get the speed needed to move any faster. I nearly collapsed over the finish line thirty seconds too late to make the time. Wow, what a disappointment. It was a hard lesson to learn.

The next time I had to do the same road march, I knew that Gatorade was not the answer for me. I powered up on water and drank only water for the entire march. That time, I didn't experience the same physical collapse near the end of the race. My body had its preferred sustenance for the journey, and I was victorious within the time limit—with some to spare. In fact, I was able to be a part of the sideline crowd cheering on the last runners. This is not a slam against Gatorade, as many of my fellow soldiers did well with Gatorade—it just didn't work for me. I didn't know what was best for me with the first road march, though I learned from the first that this option, so popular with others, was not for me.

You too will find that what is very popular with others may not be what works for you. Life is about learning and adjusting so that you still ultimately run your own race. For example, many companies are growing through mergers and acquisitions. This can be a great way to bring in new skills, competencies, and capabilities to better serve your customers. If it's the right merger or acquisition at the right time then this strategy can be very effective if the gaining organization has thought through the cultural assimilation pieces and determined how to make the merger or acquisition work. In other cases, the cultures may be too different or the timing may not be right or there may be a better way to grow. Each company has to do their own analysis to see if the strategy will work for them. Jumping on the popular bandwagon can cause harm if it's not the right bandwagon for you.

Turn No to Yes

Earlier in graduate school, when I had to make the decision about taking a job to finish my academic program, one of my major advisors was vehemently opposed to my working fulltime. Back in those days, you had to have agreement from your dissertation committee to work fulltime. My major advisor was fine with the decision; another advisor, though not thrilled, was OK with it. The third one was the hold-up. Although I was finished with my coursework and comprehensive exams and only had my research left, he felt that working would be a distraction to completing the program. We argued about the matter up one side and down the other.

"Look, I am here to complete this program and to become a psychologist," I said.

"Yes, I know, but this is not the best way," he replied.

"Well exactly what do you propose I do? The school has already said there is no funding available for this year, and my parents are not a source of financial support. So, as I see it, I have two choices: I can quit and not finish, or I can take this campus job that has been offered to me and continue my education. I'd rather continue than quit, and I can't believe you don't see the value of the choice I am making."

My advisor was silent. Finally, I said, "Tell me about when you were in graduate school. How did you make it?"

"I was married, and I had three children," he said.

I was stunned by this information. "How did you fund your education and take care of your family?"

"I worked fulltime. My parents weren't able to help me either."

"OK, so you worked fulltime and that's how you got through graduate school. Then you know it's possible to do."

"It was very difficult."

"Yes, I am sure it was difficult, and the bottom line is that you did it. Now I am just asking for my opportunity to do the same. Everything in my life has been difficult, but I still did it. You of all people should understand, given your history. Unlike some of my colleagues here, I come from a family of modest means. Not working may be an option for them, but it isn't for me. Also, in my case, I am almost finished."

Finally, he relented and approved the request for me to work. Although this was not the typical path, it was the next step in my race—in my own set of circumstances not necessarily parallel to others.

As a leader you will run into many circumstances where the answer is "no" or the door is closed. "No" is not the last word. You will have to advocate for yourself and for your people. One of my clients was the global operations manager for an upscale, niche, retail business. His company was looking for ways to be more profitable and to create worldwide synergies across the company. In an effort to standardize operations, the executive team announced some new policies. The executives had made their decisions without considering the impact on my client's business, and they had not sought his input.

In the long term, the proposed change in procedures would have destroyed the upscale niche business that the global manager and his team had worked so hard to create and make successful. Although the changes may have been beneficial for the routine clients of the business, he was certain that the distinctive approach he had created over the years was essential to retaining his high-end customer base. Loss of this line of business would likely result in significant financial loss, the very outcome the company wanted to prevent.

We showed the global operations manager how to reposition himself as a strategic thought leader with relevant information and input. Since the decisions had already been made and announced by corporate, he initially believed the situation was hopeless. Nevertheless, he created and presented a business case that showed the financial, cultural, and historical information relevant to retaining and growing his line of business and the risks of failing to continue what was working well

The executive team immediately implemented the global manager's recommendations for the high-end niche business. Both he and his team were retained in the company as valuable assets. When we first met, he'd thought his only option was to quit and find another job outside of the company and to help his people successfully land on their feet elsewhere.

This case shows that influence can happen at all stages and that leaders at all levels of the business have unique expertise that may need to be heard. With creativity and possibility thinking, leaders can make a difference even when it seems the doors are all closed. We showed this leader how to access that possibility thinking more quickly and then to execute in a way that got favorable results. This leader turned "no" to "yes."

It's Not Just About You—Others Are Watching

Running your own race is also about knowing what motivates you. When I was taking longer than my peers to complete my PhD, one of my colleagues started talking to me about how more than 50 percent of those who start PhDs do not finish them—and lots of other depressing statistics. My colleague didn't know my backstory and the steps I'd already taken to get this far. My colleague didn't know that my grandmother was already saying, "OK baby, when are you going to finish that book?"—Her term for my dissertation. "Make sure you finish it before I die." I too wanted my grandmother to see me finish my PhD.

It was a beautiful sunny day in Connecticut when my family and I traveled to the university for my graduation. I almost didn't attend, as many don't come back once they leave school and I could just as easily have received my degree in the mail. Although not the focus of this chapter, let me say that celebration is a very important part of the leadership equation. When your people have worked long and hard to achieve something, take the time to celebrate. Well, this was my time to celebrate after having worked long and hard.

My mother, my father, my grandmother, my two brothers, and my sister were all there for the occasion. It was a ceremony for all the master's and PhD recipients at the University of Connecticut in Storrs. As I scanned the audience, I saw many African-American students and their families there for master's degrees; however, I didn't see even one other African-American graduating with a doctorate.

The African-American families who were there also became members of my extended family. All day long, people I didn't know came to shake my hand.

"Congratulations. We are so proud of you," they'd say. It was the most amazing day imaginable with so much "extended family."

The joy and presence of these people forever solidified in me another key motivation that I have always had, though now it was made clearer than ever. That motivation was to do well not only for myself and my family, but also for those watching—others who might be inspired to pursue their own visions for the future. I became keenly aware of the responsibility and benefit of being part of a group that will celebrate with you, even though they don't know you, because on some level they too are you. My achievement is not mine alone, but theirs. You are leading even when you don't know it. People are watching you and drawing inspiration from what you do.

One of my clients is a senior executive in an academic setting. Although the academic setting can be informal with respect to dress, my client made a conscious effort to wear business attire to work most days and business casual on other days. What he didn't know was the extent to which the young male graduate students were both watching and emulating him as a role model for the work places they would enter upon graduation. As my client kept getting feedback about the extent to which the young males saw him as a role model, he became even more conscious and deliberate about his choices. They were watching him, and he wanted to give his best.

Lessons Learned

1. Run your own race.
2. Focus on your own destination.
3. Know your strengths and development needs, and create strategies for your best success.

Questions to Ask Yourself

1. When have I had to run my own race in a way that differed from others? What did I learn?

2. When have I mistakenly gone the way of the masses when my own journey was unique? What were the prices/consequences to be paid?

3. What's happening right now for me personally or the organization I lead that requires a unique race? What might I need to implement and how will I stay focused?

Chapter Three

Forge Your Own Pathway

"Some of the Tastiest Meals are Made from Blizzard Food"

Create Your Own Opportunity Through Service

While stationed at West Point as the clinical director of the cadet counseling center, I met the man I would marry. By the time we wed, he was stationed in Germany while I was still at West Point. It was then I made the decision to leave active military service so we could be together. Although there was some institutional effort to station dual career Army couples together, there was no guarantee. Most likely, just as my husband, Greg, returned to the US, I'd be sent overseas. I arrived in Wiesbaden, Germany on Christmas Eve as my newlywed husband's Christmas present. Now a civilian, I had to decide what work to do in this new country.

In our "stairwell"—the moniker for the type of apartment-like quarters where we lived—and the surrounding American military community, there were lots of well-educated and talented spouses who could not find work. Many of us got together to socialize while our husbands were at work. Sometimes we also spent considerable time complaining about the lack of job opportunities. But we did have the time to take tours in and around Germany and Europe to see and learn about other people and places.

Because upon arrival I only knew three words of German—*guten Tag* (hello), *danke schön* (thank you), and *auf Wiedersehen* (goodbye)—I decided to take German classes at night. I also decided to see what was happening at the American military hospital in Frankfurt. When I contacted the 97th General

Hospital in Frankfurt, I discovered that a psychologist colleague from my Walter Reed days was chief of the service. I planned to visit him to learn about opportunities for me at the hospital.

To get to Frankfurt, I had to take the train from Wiesbaden. Because I hadn't started my German class yet, my ability to negotiate the trip and understand all the rules and practices was limited. Upon arrival at the *bahnhof* (train station), I attempted to get a ticket from one of the machines. The station attendant, who was unusually patient for a German man, did not speak English and I did not speak German. He was incredibly helpful and used sign language to tell me to meet him back at the ticket kiosk at a slightly later time. I later learned that if you buy your ticket too early, it may time out as if you were trying to cheat the system—so timing was important.

At the designated time, I met the attendant at the ticket machine, purchased my ticket, and after many expressions of *danke schön*, was headed to Frankfurt. Once at the 97th General Hospital in Frankfurt, my colleague gave me a tour and explained his work. Although there were no job opportunities available for psychologists at the hospital, I asked if I could volunteer one day a week just to keep my skills sharp. He agreed, and thus began my preparation for what would be my next job.

My colleague was chief of the psychology service for the Exceptional Family Member Program. He was part of a multidisciplinary team that evaluated developmentally delayed children who had been medically evacuated to the 97th General from all over Europe, Africa, and the Middle East. The 97th General was the Walter Reed Army Medical Center of the European Region, so we got the difficult and most baffling cases that couldn't be treated locally. Trained as an adult psychologist, I was learning something completely new; we had to engage children from birth to pre-teens to evaluate their progress on significant developmental milestones.

Because many of the other team members—the developmental pediatrician, audiologist, occupational therapist, physical therapist, and speech therapist—had to perform more invasive or disturbing tests, the psychologist usually did an evaluation first before the children got into a cranky mood. My colleague was very skilled at this work, and he had tremendous rapport with children, so I learned a lot.

About three months into my weekly train commute, I saw the German bahnhof attendant who had helped me on my first day. By this time, I had learned a few more words of German, so I went up to him and reminded him of who I was before carrying on a full conversation in broken German. He was amazed and delighted as he remembered when I didn't speak any German. My only agenda was to express my deep appreciation for his help on that first day, to let him know how important he was, and to encourage his attitude of helpfulness toward others. He was beaming when I left him that day. I too was thrilled to see that I had learned enough German to speak with him so that he could understand me. This conversation was a test, proof that I was learning German.

After six months of taking the train from Wiesbaden to Frankfurt to volunteer at the hospital once a week, my colleague got orders to transfer to another duty station back in the United States. There were no active duty psychologists available to fill his slot. The EMFP program was considered important and they didn't want to lose their psychologist input. I was asked if I was interested in the job. This was an unexpected and fabulous opportunity. For me to be allowed to take the job, it had to be temporarily converted to a civilian government position. My colleague, along with others, did all the necessary paperwork and got me set up to serve in the role.

Once the change was made, our department was moved from the hospital to a separate facility in a small community on the outskirts of Frankfurt. I was now driving to Frankfurt—a much better commute so far as parking and being integrated into the community was concerned. I had lots of opportunities to practice my German when going to lunch in the neighborhood.

So there I was, chief of the psychology service for the EFM Program, which included Frankfurt, Giessen, and Hanau. I recruited another psychologist to staff the Hanau clinic. In our new location, I had to learn yet another skill: how to work in front of other professionals. In the past, each of the disciplines performed their work separately and then came together for a joint case conference to share findings and determine patient dispositions. Also, historically, psychologists worked privately with clients behind closed doors. I learned yet a tremendous amount more and came to truly value the power of a multidisciplinary team. I happily held this job for a year before my husband and I transferred to Montgomery, Alabama.

The point of this story is that sometimes you make your own opportunities, which may necessitate viewing less than ideal circumstances as your next (beneficial) step. Commuting by train to Frankfurt was inconvenient and working with children was not on my bucket list, but I was wired to serve and add value and that volunteer opportunity provided both. In return, I received a priceless education and a very good job for the rest of my time in Germany. What a blessing!

As a leader, you may have the opportunity to serve on a company board, to volunteer your services with a local nonprofit organization, or to serve on a committee or task-force in your company. These acts of service benefit both your company and the other end user beneficiaries. At the same time, you are developing and honing new skills and abilities to be used both now and later. You may have no idea how these skills will be useful; however, when you serve, the benefit is always in both directions.

Build on Previous Learning and Take the Next Step

As we were about to move to Alabama, I sent a letter to the chief of the mental health department of Air Regional Hospital at Maxwell Air Force Base to let him know I would be coming to the area and to see what new opportunities I could create. My husband was scheduled to attend an Air Force officer school instead of the Army equivalent as previously planned.

The chief of the service wrote back and asked me to schedule an appointment to meet with him when I got there. At our first meeting, he remarked on the depth of my experience and background. I learned about a program in the hospital where independent professionals agreed to see military families at the hospital; in return for physical office space and scheduling support, the providers agreed to charge a slightly lower fee than usual.

The chief was really interested in having me in the clinic because they needed someone to work with children. Although this was a more standard child and family therapy practice as opposed to an evaluation clinic like the EFMP, my experience in Germany was a very helpful stepping stone to this job. A year later, when we were about to transfer to another duty assignment, I had already built a full and thriving practice that I was able to transfer to the provider who came along after me.

Leaders are builders. As a leader you will have the opportunity to leave things better than you found them and to provide resources for others. Remember to leave a path, trail, or bustling highway for others behind you to travel more easily to their destinations. You are only a leader if someone is following. When enough people create new pathways, the network of roads and destinations is endless.

Embrace new learning. You never know how it will benefit you in the future. Some doors open only because you have already availed yourself of a prior learning opportunity and thus are prepared to take on greater responsibilities.

Each Step Leads Closer to Your Ultimate Vision

Having now landed on my feet a couple of times since my active duty Army days, I was about to repeat the same formula for Colorado Springs. Only this time, I called on two specific colleagues, both Air Force psychologists who were at the US Air Force Academy while I was at West Point. I met them when they came to visit us to exchange ideas for operating at service academies.

Both psychologists were now retired from the Air Force. One was in private practice in town and both were working at the Center for Creative Leadership (CCL), a world-class and top-ten ranked executive leadership development training organization. The one in private practice was an adjunct executive coach and feedback consultant at CCL; the other had a part-time faculty appointment there. I started a private practice at the same location as my private practice colleague. He had space and was looking for more providers. In the meantime, the part-time faculty member invited me to visit CCL on what I thought was an informal visit. As it turned out, I met the local director, was interviewed, and ultimately offered a job at CCL.

I was very excited about the opportunity at CCL because while in the Army and especially at the First Infantry Division at Fort Riley, Kansas, I was very intrigued by the impact of leadership effectiveness on soldier experience and mental health. In my role as division psychologist, I attended to both leadership and clinical issues. It was in the Army that I first had a vision of applying psychological principles to leadership and the workplace. CCL offered the opportunity I sought to test my hand at leadership development. I spent my first few months as an adjunct coach and feedback consultant and then I was recruited in-house as a senior faculty member and as the chief assessor who managed all the adjunct coaches for the Colorado office.

CCL was a steep learning curve for me because coaching is not the same as therapy and training is not the same as teaching. Though it took me a while to figure out how best to apply my prior knowledge and experience, I ultimately figured it out. Eventually I became a go-to person for difficult coaching cases where someone with good skills and instincts was needed or in cases where clients were not satisfied and their coaching sessions had to be redone. My ability to listen, connect with my clients, and see the connections or opportunities they didn't readily see is what made me successful.

One week, while conducting an open enrollment course for the Leadership Development Program, one of our local TV news anchors was in attendance. Toward the end of the week, she asked if I had ever considered doing television. She gave me her card and told me to give her a call. She and her husband were local team anchors on the morning news. After a few conversations, they invited me to appear on the program to talk about child and family psychology issues. After the first show, they asked me to be a regular weekly guest, which I did for several years.

The show was live and my segment, called "Ask Dr. Karen," aired on Monday mornings and was promoted over the weekend by announcing whatever topic I was going to address. People called in live to the show with their questions, and it was a lot of fun to answer, educate, and help in the moment. People in the community recognized me at the mall or local restaurants and said, "Oh, you are Dr. Karen. I watch your show every week. You have really helped me help my daughter with our grandson Johnny." I loved doing this program because I could reach so many people who otherwise would never come to a psychologist's office.

On the training side, I eventually became known as a great coach, teacher, facilitator, and mentor to new faculty. CCL was a fast-moving train, and at the time I joined there was not much help in the way of training prep—you either sank or swam on your own. The Colorado office was a lean start-up organization, and you had to be independent and self-reliant. Later, as the office grew, more intentionality was placed on training and mentoring inexperienced staff members.

I often say that I was like a golf coach who knows the fundamentals of the game, can teach them to someone else, and can study their technique and help them to hone it for further excellence. Like a good elite golf coach, my students were often more skilled than me at training and they became Tiger Woods in their own right. Over the years, many successful CCL colleagues told me stories of lessons I taught them that made all the difference in their development and ultimate excellence. As always, I was functioning in my core skill, which is consulting.

One day while at CCL, my co-trainer and I were working with a custom client, a team of colleagues that worked together at the same company. We were delivering a training program designed to meet their leadership development needs. The client wanted more free space and open time to deal with specific organizational issues; however, we had to get the training done. As a consultant, I could see what we needed to do, though it would mean somewhat diverging from the planned agenda. As a 501(c)(3) education and training nonprofit organization, CCL was constrained from doing true consulting.

With some creativity and ingenuity, I created an intervention that was a bit less education and training oriented in its approach, which I led with the company after lunch. My training partners observed. When we got to the end of the intervention, the client was happy and my CCL colleagues were amazed. It was then that I realized anew that my signature gift was more aligned with consulting than training. This was an important epiphany that led to my next move.

After almost five years in my two primary roles at CCL as senior faculty and chief assessor, I decided to start my own company, TRANSLEADERSHIP, INC., and to join the on-call faculty at CCL, where I still enjoy a great relationship with wonderful colleagues and clients. Starting TRANSLEADERSHIP,

INC. allowed me to return to my entrepreneurial roots as a business owner and to operate more frequently in my core gift of consulting. Two years after starting TRANSLEADERSHIP, I also closed my part-time private practice and went 100 percent fulltime into the business application of psychology.

As a leader, every job and every life experience you have makes you a richer source of empathy, understanding, and knowledge for a wider variety of leadership experiences. Your unique tapestry weaves together many separate strands to create a beautiful masterpiece. The resourcefulness and creativity you called upon to take each step can be used again to create yet another masterpiece. Stepping out and forging your own pathway creates the confidence to do it again even if the territory is new. Each experience sharpens your focus about what you like, your unique gifts and talents, and what might be next.

Summary Thoughts on Forging Your Own Pathway

This chapter is about recognizing opportunities and options and creating your own path forward even if what you are looking at resembles "blizzard food"—a concept I coined for those days when you haven't gone grocery shopping and an unexpected blizzard pops up. The weather is too severe to go to the store, so you must search an empty refrigerator and pantry and find food anyway. I remember one such occasion when I had downsized all the food out of the refrigerator and the pantry in anticipation of having the caterer fill the refrigerator with food for seventy guests for my husband's military retirement party. His parents had flown in from Washington state and it was the night before the party, which also happened to be my husband's birthday. On this birthday Friday, a huge blizzard unexpectedly sprung up. I barely made it home from work.

The restaurant we planned to go to that evening for my husband's birthday celebration said they were closing early. I found a driver willing to go to the restaurant to pick up the dinner and my husband's birthday cake. They sent the food on real plates and that night we had a great dinner and birthday celebration. It snowed all night and by the next day we had four feet of snow—everything was canceled. We had to postpone the retirement party until the next weekend. The caterer didn't come, the refrigerator was empty, and my in-laws were visiting. I searched the empty refrigerator and near empty cabinets and discovered food I ordinarily would have looked right past. For the next several days, I prepared blizzard food. Sometimes life is like that: we open the doors, windows, and closets, we don't see the blizzard food that's in there, and we certainly wouldn't think about cooking and serving it—yet some of the tastiest meals are made from blizzard ingredients. The blizzard food is right in front of us if we are willing to see with new eyes.

Although I have been talking about blizzard food as overlooked opportunities, blizzard food may also be overlooked people in your organization—those people you don't see or even consider when you open the pantry or refrigerator, yet who could be part of creating a tasty meal for your organization. Some may need a little salt, pepper, garlic, or other seasoning to be ready for prime time. Others just need to be combined with the right other ingredients for success. You have food that will sustain your organization and help it to grow. Remember to see and utilize your stored food to its best benefit. Don't wait for a blizzard to see what assets are available to you.

Lessons Learned

1. Access and add to your network on a regular basis.
2. Look for opportunities in the far-reaching corners of your current experiences.
3. See each experience and opportunity as a learning tool to prepare you for even greater future opportunities.

Questions to Ask Yourself

1. What blizzard food have I found in my life? What gourmet food was I able to create with the blizzard food?

2. What career pieces have I been able to put together from unexpected opportunities or options I created for myself?

3. How can I show others how to access these same resources in their own lives?

Bonus Content

For some thoughts on how to season your people with ingredients for success, watch my video, "Top Ten Tips for Leading High Performance Teams that Get Dynamic Organizational Results."

Go to

http://transleadership.com/resources/team-video1/

Chapter Four

Focus on the Positive

"Let's Make Gutter Balls Winning Balls"

Focus on What You Want

"How many times do I have to tell you to be more careful and to stop dropping those glasses!" my mother yelled.

Somehow, I had gotten labeled as clumsy. Even though I didn't fundamentally think I was clumsy, I certainly was now acting like it. With the drinking glass clutched tightly in my two hands, walking slowly across the room with eyes riveted on the glass, I yet again tripped, dropped the glass, and broke it. I felt hopeless and doomed to failure in those moments. My mother's yelling only served to reinforce this negative assessment of myself. Do you know how hard it is to drive in a straight line if your eyes are riveted to the hood of the car rather than to the place in the distance you want to drive? That's how I felt in childhood.

No matter how much I concentrated on perfect walking with the glass, something always happened that kept my mind repeatedly creating what I didn't want. I behaviorally figured it out though my mind didn't catch up to the discovery until many years later. Finally, giving up on being able to carry glasses to my mother's satisfaction, I finally said to myself, "Forget it. If they break they break. I don't care anymore." And, once I stopped caring about breaking glasses, I stopped breaking glasses. I didn't see this victory right away. My behavioral change at that time was rooted in "giving up," though the real reason it worked was that I was no longer focused on breaking glasses.

In the fourth grade, my friend Emily and I spent a lot of time in the outfield praying that no balls would come our way. No one wanted us on their athletic team, nor did we want to be on anyone's team. We enjoyed talking to one another while dodging balls like incoming artillery. By the time I got out of elementary school, I was convinced that I had no talent for sports. Most of the messages I'd received from peers were negative. My go-to strategy was to avoid any semblance of sports. As I later entered high school, the only sports I pursued were individual sports where I competed with myself for better times at the 100-yard dash or again with myself about how much weight I could bench-press. Girls didn't take weight training back then, so I was the only girl in the class. Whenever I had a choice, I always opted out of team sports because I tired of the negativity.

One day when I was in college, I came home to visit my family and I attended my father's company barbecue with him. When we arrived at the barbecue, they were playing baseball and were delighted we had arrived because they needed two more team members. I flat out refused to play and told them all the reasons they didn't want me on their team. I made it clear that I couldn't hit and I couldn't catch. They claimed they didn't care about this track record—they just wanted me to play. We argued back and forth for a while, me making dire warnings that they'd be sorry to have me on their team. With much trepidation, I finally agreed to play.

"Strike" the catcher called when I was first at bat. I was ready for the verbal beatings and berating; however, my father's colleagues said nothing but positive things. They encouraged me and said, "Way to go for swinging at the ball," etc. They found something right to reinforce in every move, no matter the outcome. If they thought that a helpful tip might help in how I held the bat or any other move, then they offered that all in a positive, can-do approach. Not once did they say anything negative, no matter what I did. This was certainly different. Next thing I knew, the bat contacted the ball and I had a base hit, then another hit, and we were off to the races. The more they encouraged me, the better I played.

"Wait, we thought you couldn't play!" they said.

"I have never played like this, ever," I said.

We laughed, cheered everyone, and genuinely had fun. That day I played the best baseball of my life, and I even caught some balls in the outfield. No one was more shocked than me. What I learned and realized that day was the true power of positive reinforcement. From their positive words, coaching, and celebration, my teammates shaped my behavior to its best performance. The transformation was immediate and very visible. What I realized for the first time that day was that I didn't have a fundamental inability to play sports—rather, a constant barrage of negative feedback had me focusing on what I couldn't do, just like my mother's negative comments about dropping glasses.

The Power of Positive Reinforcement

I had grown up in a school culture that only provided punishment for imperfect athletics. What if they had encouraged me and shaped my behavior with a positive can-do approach? Perhaps I wouldn't have grown up hating and avoiding team sports. Punishment is providing a negative consequence for behavior you want to stop. If a child touches a hot stove, the parent might slap the child's hand to prevent that behavior in the future. Punishment halts behavior. In the past, when I got verbal slaps for not catching balls in the outfield, I stopped catching balls in the outfield. Use punishment sparingly and only for the most dangerous "hot stove" situations that need to be stopped immediately, because punishment does not encourage or inspire desired behavior—it just discourages the behavior being punished.

Positive reinforcement, on the other hand, is providing a positive consequence for behavior you want to increase, so when my father's work colleagues provided cheers and positive affirmations for all approximations of hitting and catching balls, I hit and caught more balls. This principle is very simple; however, most schools and workplaces use punishment when the outcomes they want are more likely to occur with positive reinforcement.

Much later in life, I went to New Jersey with some colleagues for a training job. The hotel where we stayed had two bowling lanes in the basement. My colleagues were mostly mountain climbers and avid skiers. None of them were bowlers or had any real skill bowling, so we decided to bowl with a twist.

"Let's make gutter balls winning balls," someone said.

"Yeah, that's a clever idea. Let's do it. Every time someone hits a gutter ball, we will cheer."

Early in the game, there were lots of gutter balls. We cheered, celebrated, and laughed our rear ends off. People got points for gutter balls. We also cheered strikes and spares too. Before long, people were playing well, and it was the most fun I have ever had bowling, prior or since.

Over the years, my parents convened frequently with one another to talk about what I was doing next. The subject could be about me traveling to a dangerous country to work, going on a military assignment that seemed daunting, or taking a job that no one expected me to take. Invariably, my mother spoke to my father about all the dangers inherent in my next choice. No matter how outlandish my next step or plan seemed, my father always said, "Karen will be fine. She can do anything she sets her mind to do." My mother interpreted my father's comments as not caring. In my mother's economy, caring meant worrying. They both cared. My mother just got scared when she couldn't see the "how." My father, on the other hand, kept calling out the pattern he had seen play out repeatedly in my life. Years later, I better saw the value of my father's gift of calling out my strength, vision, and resilience. His spoken confidence in me encouraged me to succeed in many challenges.

In spite of her worries, my mother was the true risk-taker and entrepreneur. Over the years she dabbled with businesses that included dress making, cake baking, and a laundry service.

She was also my role model for taking uncommon action and doing different things. For example, she was the first woman I ever saw drive a mail truck at a time when women weren't doing that job. An excellent speaker and conversationalist, people were easily drawn to her. My father was the stable, quiet, and more conventional person. He modeled excellence, patience, hard work, and persistence. These qualities enabled him to repeatedly get identified for promotion and greater responsibility.

What if you led by always thinking about how you could inspire, encourage, and reinforce more of what you were looking for from your employees? I once worked with a leader who was having a challenging time building a high-performance team. The leader before him had been one of those shepherds who always beat the sheep. The employees learned not to trust leadership; no matter what style the new leader used, they kept waiting for the beating. His employees were conditioned to expect the worst and were perpetually waiting for the "I told you so" moment. In the meantime, my client was tearing his hair out.

It wasn't enough for him to just be behaviorally different from their past leader—he had to change the norms and expectations of his group. They had to make new agreements with one another and collectively set a new agenda. There is a Bible verse that says, "There is no fear in love. But perfect love drives out fear, because fear has to do with punishment. The one who fears is not made perfect in love" (I John 4:18, NIV). Over time he was able to heal past wounds and to consistently show that he was a leader who supported and loved his followers.

In many ways, his team acted like foster children who had been passed around from home to home. Though they wanted a real home, they acted as if that wasn't important to them. Fearful of being rejected, they acted in all the ways that would ensure their rejection. Thus, the same pattern kept playing out on the stage of their work lives. Until those foster children encounter a family who refuses to be frightened off by their antics and instead loves them through the pain and trauma, they will continue to bounce from family to family. My client had to show he had the kind of love that could put up with their imperfections and that would inspire them to their best work. Again, this took time and many deliberate actions on his part. He had to pass the foster children's test with a strategic blend of both love and boundaries.

Lessons Learned

1. Encourage and reinforce what you want, and you will get more of what you want.
2. Use strengths as your foundation for success. Identify and build on "what's right" with this picture.
3. See mistakes as positive learning opportunities.

Questions to Ask Yourself

1. What punishment do I need to stop before I can care for my team more perfectly?
2. What additional opportunities for positive reinforcement can I identify in my workplace? What will this encouragement look like day-to-day?
3. How can I encourage and support myself to be a better leader?

Chapter Five

Build Strength, Fortitude, and Confidence through Challenges

"Face Fears and Do It Anyway"

Face Your Greatest Fear

One of the reasons I loved school is that I enjoy intellectual challenges, which excite and intrigue me. As a Girl Scout cadet, I had badges down the front and all the way up the back of my sash. I was very achievement-oriented.

However, I was not so enthused about physical challenges, despite being a hardcore Girl Scout. In addition to routine easy scouting, I also did the kind where we dug our own firepits for cooking, pitched Army-like pup tents, and used temporary latrines. My mother always said that scouting prepared me for the Army. Like a prairie woman from days gone by, I'd show up in a dress and could do anything I needed to while wearing it. Except for having to avoid bats at night, scouting was fun.

Despite this early exposure to outdoor adventures, I was apprehensive, knowing the Army took outdoor living to a whole new level. The kinds of challenges we faced in the Army were unlike anything I had ever seen before. One thing I knew prior to joining the Army was that I had no interest in rappelling, which was featured in lots of ROTC commercials. When I told the hardcore Army recruiter captain that this kind of activity was not for me, he said, "Oh, no, as a psychologist, you won't have to rappel."

As I stood there looking up at the twenty-five-foot rappelling tower, I thought back to the captain's words. Not only would I indeed have to rappel, but also perform many other physical challenges they hadn't mentioned. My intern colleagues from Walter Reed and I were "observing" and participating in the enlisted basic training exercise, namely the Army Confidence Course at Fort Campbell in Kentucky. We had just finished the briefing on how to climb the stairs to the top of the rappelling tower wall, how to hook on the equipment with various carabiners, and the role of the belay master who ostensibly would not let us fall. We even saw demonstrations of someone being safely suspended in midair by the belay master, so this exercise was supposedly 100 percent safe. That's also what I'd been told in high school on the uneven parallel bars, though my spotters dropped me anyway and I ended up with a concussion. And this was much higher up and far more daunting than gymnastics.

I was the last one to go up. Everyone before me had survived, and they were now heading to the fifty-foot tower. All of this was practice for being on real mountains (hills) that afternoon. Well, there was no further delaying, since I was last. I thought to myself, "Just how hard could it be?" I had no idea that it would be even more daunting than I imagined.

I started up the stairs to the top of the tower. I wasn't overly afraid of heights, and from the ground it didn't seem to be too bad; however, the higher I climbed, the more frightened I became because the stairs were straight up and down. There was no gentle grade like you have on a normal staircase. I didn't even know in advance what such stairs would feel like. Now not only did I have the rappelling to worry about, but also just getting there.

Finally, I made it to the top of the tower wall where a sergeant was waiting. He gave me the rope and I connected the harness as previously instructed; however, I proceeded to forget everything else. Standing at the top of the wall, I attempted to hold all my weight with the rope—which is not what you are supposed to do.

The sergeant said, "Captain, let go of the rope."

"No, if I let go I am going to fall."

"No, you won't fall. There's the belay master on the ground holding the other end of the rope."

Nothing appeared as we had practiced it. Everything was much worse than I had imagined, and my mind had already imagined the worst—or so I thought. I was holding all my weight with the rope. This was an unsustainable position as I weighed too much for this type of feat and holding myself up was exhausting. I felt terrorized and convinced I would ultimately plunge to my death.

"I've changed my mind. I am going back down," I said.

"Oh yes, you are going down: by way of rappelling down the wall," the sergeant said. "You cannot get past me to the stairs, so let go of the rope." Finally, in exhaustion, I composed myself long enough to reluctantly ease up on the rope and rappel down the wall. It was a small though monumental victory. I knew I wasn't ready for the fifty-foot tower, so I stayed at the twenty-five and rappelled down it a few more times until I was no longer afraid. Then I proceeded to the fifty-foot tower and rappelled down it a couple of times until I felt I had mastered that challenge. Later in the afternoon, I was fine for the real mountains and hills. I had done the one thing I most feared doing.

The sergeant at the top of the twenty-five-foot tower wall was very important to my success. When I didn't believe in myself or the equipment and was ready to give up, he wouldn't let me quit. Had he allowed me to go back down the tower by way of the stairs, I never would have conquered my fear or any of those rappelling challenges. Had I been allowed to walk back down, I would never have set foot on another rappelling platform in my life. He believed in me, in the training, and in the equipment when I did not. As a result, I overcame my fears and succeeded.

We often need sergeants at the tops of life's difficult walls: those who will call out the best in us and remind us of the supports and resources at our disposal. These are the people who won't let us stop short of our goals. In the moment, I was not appreciative of him or his role; I only wanted to turn back.

Only after I rappelled down the wall did I appreciate him for removing this fear and barrier from my life.

When you dream big dreams, there will be daunting rappelling wall challenges. The sergeant at the top of the wall is there to remind you of your forward-moving vision and to prevent any backsliding. You can do it, even if you temporarily think you can't. The belay master on the ground is the safety. Even if something were to go terribly wrong, he can yank the rope and stop you in midair. Though the exercise feels dangerous, lots of safety is built into the system. The feeling of risk and danger is far worse than the actuality. In life, it's also good to have that safety person on the ground ready to be your guardian angel if needed. You can experiment with a lot of new behavior with a sergeant and belay master on board to help.

Sometimes, however, the reality of a situation is much worse than you anticipated. In those moments, you rely on your support people, training, and other help. Real life can be more daunting than what we've practiced or imagined. Even when that's the case, there is still a way to proceed through the challenge. As the Army is fond of saying, "adapt and overcome." I also learned that—like the Nike slogan—"just doing it" helps to conquer fear. Sometimes you do it more than once to get the confidence needed to move forward because repetition increases comfort and skill. Then you proceed to the next challenge. There is a reason they called it the Army Confidence Course.

Establish Credibility—Do Hard Things

The most difficult challenge I pursued in the Army was going out for the Expert Field Medical Badge (EFMB), the highest achievement of the Army Medical Department. I was with the 1st Medical Battalion of the First Infantry Division at Fort Riley, Kansas. The infantry troops had a highly coveted and respected Expert Infantryman's Badge (EIB), and the EFMB was the Army's Medical Department equivalent. As a young psychologist in an infantry division, I felt I needed something more substantial in my credentials to demonstrate my military capabilities. Infantrymen did not necessarily value or respect psychologists; however, they did value the EFMB, especially those who were saved by medics in Viet Nam. Those who performed medical heroics in combat received the Combat EFMB.

The requirements included taking a written test of medical knowledge such as how to triage patients, purify water, load a medevac helicopter, survive a gas attack, and much more. In addition to the written test, there was a three-hour, twelve-mile, forced road march with a full eighty-pound duffle bag of field gear (see Chapter Three for a fuller description of this exercise), and one week in the field (woods) engaging in a variety of medical tests under challenging conditions, time constraints, and simulated enemy attacks. The whole exercise was mentally, physically, and emotionally draining.

Most soldiers were worried about the written test. The intellectual part was the least of my concerns, since academic achievement was my go-to. At the beginning of the process we had 300 people who decided to compete for the EFMB. After the written test, half had flunked out, so now 150 people went on to the twelve-mile forced road march. After the march, those who successfully made the time continued to the week-long field simulation. There were multiple stations set up in the woods to test our skills at being medics. If you failed at any station, then you were sent home. Every day, the numbers kept dwindling until the final day when only about thirty of us remained—of those, only a very small handful were women, including a nurse and a lieutenant in my unit. Of all my Army accolades, the EFMB is the one of which I am most proud. I worked hard to achieve it and wear it proudly on my uniform.

Afterward, whenever I showed up to an infantry or field artillery unit wearing the EFMB, I received instant respect. Though I may not have looked tough, they knew I had to be to obtain this badge. Again, here was something I set my mind to do and I persisted until it was done. Rising to and meeting challenges produces confidence and skill. You find out that you can do more than you ever thought possible. Having already successfully met challenges, I was undaunted by taking the next hill. I had already succeeded against great odds and knew I could do it again.

Summary Thoughts on Building Strength, Fortitude, and Confidence Through Challenges

Sometimes I am the sergeant at the top of the wall or the belay master on the ground for my clients. I cheer them on and let them know they can go another mile on the twelve-mile road march. Sometimes, I run alongside them providing inspiration and encouragement, knowing they can make it through. I see their greatness and call it out in them. Having been through many tests and trials myself, I know that what looks impossible is truly possible. We develop and implement strategies, evaluate progress, and plan our next moves.

In one case, I was working with a female executive who was newly promoted to her high-level position in an academic setting. Her boss was a woman from the old school who did not have the benefit of formal leadership development. My client, on the other hand, had been exposed to top-notch leadership training. She knew what a senior leader was supposed to provide to the organization and she knew her boss was not providing any of it. Her boss was a micromanager who tried to run everything and make every decision herself. Unfortunately, on her own, the boss did not have all the information she needed to make the best decisions—though that did not stop her from making many decisions that proved onerous for the team.

The rest of the organization had grown accustomed to the boss's interference and most of them had been silenced many years ago. My client was new to this system and couldn't understand their passivity. The boss also had a reputation for killing the messenger, and my client's peers had witnessed many hangings over the years. Although my client's peers really appreciated her fresh voice, insights, and ideas about how to move forward, they would only make supportive comments to her privately and outside of meetings with the boss. If anyone was to be axed, they planned on being far from the boss's aim.

For my client, this environment was like rappelling off the wall and not knowing if there was a belay master. Over the course of our time together, we crafted strategies that allowed her to step into her own senior leadership shoes and speak truth to power. She didn't get the axe, and ultimately both her peers and boss came to value the wisdom and leadership she brought to the institution. Although unstated, the boss saw my client as the heir apparent to take her job when she retired in a year. She was looking for someone with the courage of her convictions. My client fit the bill. She just needed some help reframing her view of her circumstances, so she could then rappel down that wall.

Lessons Learned

1. Face your fears and do it anyway.
2. Surround yourself with people who challenge you, won't let you give up, and who also support you.
3. Practice and repeat an action until the fear goes away and you develop the skill.

Questions to Ask Yourself

1. What have I learned from persisting through fears that I can share with someone else?
2. In what ways has my confidence and skill level been expanded by the challenges I have faced and overcome?
3. What am I now avoiding that I just need to do? Whom can I enlist as my sergeant and belay master?

Chapter Six

Learn from Others

"Grow and Go"

Invest in Yourself

The best investment you can make is in yourself. I have always been a continuous learner—even with a PhD, I don't see myself as being done with learning. So long as I am living and contributing on the planet there will be a need to learn, grow, and go. The world is constantly changing, and you need a mindset of continuous learning to keep up. I am the instrument of my leadership, and you are yours. You lead from who you have developed yourself to be. In addition, the flaws in your leadership reflect learning yet to take place.

As a licensed psychologist, I am required to take approximately thirty hours per year of continuing education. Prior to this requirement, I took thirty hours a year anyway just because I wanted to keep up with the latest information and to show up as my best when working with my clients. Two conferences I regularly attend are the annual Midwinter Conference (MWC) (now named the Consulting Psychology Conference [CPC]) of the Society of Consulting Psychologists and the annual American Psychological Association Convention. In addition to these conferences, I attend others on marketing, entrepreneurial business, leadership, and many other topics.

I use conference time for strategic thinking and planning my next steps. It's time I use to prime the pump and seed my thoughts with valuable reflections and insights. Sometimes what I create from these experiences goes far beyond what I heard at the conference because I am also mixing it with my own experiences and history.

I have colleagues who own their own businesses; however, they will not invest in themselves through off-site conferences.

Coming from an employee mindset, if the company does not pay the bill, then they will not go. As a business owner, the company belongs to you, so it is even easier to get to a conference than if you worked for an outside employer and had to get approval. I love being able to make whatever education decision makes strategic sense for me and my business. I also had this mindset as an employee. If my employer didn't invest in an opportunity I thought was important, then I invested in it myself.

Some of my best learning and continuing education is from books. I am always reading a book or two. Though my area of concentration at work is leadership, most of my reading is on spiritual topics as I am inspired by those whose lives also have a spiritual calling. Most of my reading is nonfiction and I love biographies and autobiographies of amazing people like Billy Graham, Mother Teresa, D. L. Moody, Andrew Murray, and George Mueller. I particularly like reading about people from times past who overcame tremendous odds to make a significant difference in the world. My friend and colleague Dr. Christopher Brooks has written many scholarly books about music greats. I particularly loved his book about Shirley Verrett, *I Never Walked Alone: The Autobiography of an American Singer* and the one about Roland Hayes, *The Legacy of an American Tenor*, which he co-wrote with Robert Sims.

Some of my other favorite books include *The Cost of Discipleship* by Dietrich Bonhoeffer, which inspired me to read his biography, *Bonhoeffer*, by Eric Metaxis—another excellent read. I also loved Viktor Frankl's *Man's Search for Meaning* and Pastor Canisius Gacura's book *Unlimited: Conquering on my Knees*. Those who have triumphed over all kinds of odds are my kind of people, and reading about them inspires me to my next work. Other books I've enjoyed include *The Wealth Choice: Success Secrets of Black Millionaires* by Dennis Kimbro; *No Excuses* and *Change Your Thinking, Change Your Life*, both by Brian Tracy; and *The Richest Man in Babylon* by George Clason. I have been greatly enriched by books—too many to list here. The point is you can go to other times, places, and worlds through books while also transforming your mind.

One of the best ways to learn something is to teach it to others. I regularly speak at professional meetings and conventions giving a variety of presentations including the following subset, "Leading High Performance Teams for Impact"; "Leading Successful and Dynamic Organizational Change"; "Influence, Collaboration, and Development Strategies for Leaders in High-Stress environments"; "Practical Strategies for Creating Collaborative Relationships in Corporate Business Environments"; "Defying Gravity to use our Best and Full Selves for Breakthrough Results"; "Coming out with our Diverse and Multiple Identities"; "Best Practices for Hiring Top Talent in Key Positions"; and "Consulting Best Practices from one Wheelhouse Over."

If you are interested in booking me to speak to your organization on one of these or other topics, go to:

http://transleadership.com/services/speaking-form/

Learn from people on your journey. Your teacher today may be the cab or limo driver, the housekeeper at the hotel, or the waiter in the restaurant. Learning opportunities abound and reside in all kinds of people and places, so be open to learning from what you think are unlikely sources.

There is a reservoir near my father's house in Baltimore. For years, he daily walked around this lake (as we called the reservoir) for exercise, and when I visited home, I'd often join him. There was an older gentleman who also occasionally walked around the lake. This man had a way with words and was wise and poetic in his expressions. In speaking about how he was talking to his daughters about principles in selecting a marriage partner, he observed that his daughters didn't realize that it took years to grow and develop a husband of high quality and character like their dad. He reminded them that if they stepped on the caterpillar, they'd never get to see the butterfly. This thought has stayed with me for many years.

Most of my best clients are also continuous learners. They want to grow and go in new directions with new insights and skills. I am their consultant because they are looking to move rather than to remain static. If you are not in a growth mode, then you are dying, and dying quickly. Consider the laws of nature: all that lives also grows and renews. Once growth and renewal stop, then death is near. You choose to grow not just for yourself, but also for your organization and those who follow your leadership. You owe it to yourself and those who follow you to provide fertile soil for growth.

Invest in Others

Keep in mind that how things look on the surface is not necessarily synonymous with their deeper structure. I remember an African violet plant I had years ago. An insect or disease had gotten hold of the plant, so it had to sit outside for a while. During this phase, the plant looked completely brown, withered, and dead. Judging by appearances, there was nothing to salvage. The average person would have thrown the plant away and called it a day. There were no visible signs of life in this plant, and although I am far from having a green thumb, I really liked the plant and its previously velvety purple leaves.

Armed with this love for what the plant had been and possibly could still be again, I started watering it. For weeks, I watered the plant with no visible sign of change. People started laughing at me for wasting water on such an undeserving plant. Many weeks later, I saw some small tender shoots emerging out of the deadness. Next thing I knew, there were more green leaves, and then velvety purple leaves. Much to even my amazement, the plant revived and went on to live many more productive years until I had to move and gift it to someone else.

Learning is like water or fertilizer to a dying plant. That which seems hopeless can be revived and made alive again. In the workplace, there are many African violet plants waiting for someone to provide that nurturing drink of water. You can be the plant doctor who speaks life into what seems lifeless, because at the core, life is still there and can be called out. Others in the workplace are green, thriving, and growing like my academic client. Pouring water on her and others like her creates a lush tropical forest because she is already alive and flourishing. However, you can only pour water on others if your own cup is full and you have water to share—hence the call to continuous learning as a leader. Keep your own cup full.

One of my clients, a corporate leader in and from India, was concerned because his team never seemed to have any ideas about what to do next. They had come to rely on him to tell them what to do and then they would implement, though not independently enough. My client wanted to lead a more empowered team that was growing and developing; however, he could not get them to speak up and follow their own thoughts and ideas. As their senior, his team saw him as having more knowledge and expertise; in their culture, it was easy for them to defer to his direction.

For this intervention, we talked about what my client was doing to inadvertently maintain the very dynamics he wanted to change and how he could begin to shift his own behavior to create a culture of learning and development. He had to create the conditions for his people to test innovative ideas and behaviors, to develop their own skills, and to stretch their dormant wings. By the time we finished our engagement, he had built a cohesive learning organization. His people were regularly sharing and implementing their own ideas, not just his. His people were happier at work, more confident, and more productive. In addition, he didn't have to be there to ensure that something got done. They became highly motivated self-starters who were enthusiastic about their work and the opportunity to contribute to the company's success and bottom line results.

Lessons Learned

1. Invest in yourself first and then also in your people and your organization.

2. Prioritize all kinds of continuous learning such as conferences, books, webinars/recordings, seminars, and training programs.

3. Learn from all kinds of people whether past or present. Those from the past are still living through the legacy of their recorded experiences.

Questions to Ask Yourself

1. From what resources am I currently learning? What am I learning from these resources?

2. What else do I need to learn, and where can I go for this learning?

3. How am I creating a continuous learning organization in my workplace? What more can I do to seed and water learning in my organization?

Chapter Seven

Feed Your Spirit

"Listen for Divine Direction and Guidance"

Get Grounded for Your Day

As a person of faith, the first substantive activity of my day is reading the Bible and spending time with God in prayer. This is a powerful start to every day as I gain wisdom, direction, and clarity even if the time spent is short. So much of vision is spiritual, beyond what I can see in the natural. When possible and available, I also spend time listening to my favorite Christian speakers on the radio, such as Dr. Charles Stanley, Dr. Todd Hudnell, Dr. Tony Evans, and Dr. David Jeremiah. Frequently as I am listening or reading, the answers to prior questions are miraculously addressed. These answers often come within forty-eight hours of having posed the question myself or having been asked the question by someone else.

Grounding my day in the spiritual also keeps me aware and listening for divine direction and guidance. There have been many times when I have been divinely guided to speak to a client about something I wasn't planning to say, yet which was relevant. Sometimes these moments happen on airplanes with people I don't know, yet God has a word for them, and on that day, I am the vessel. I call these "divine appointments." I never know when I might have a divine appointment, so staying spiritually connected is key because I may be deployed that day to speak hope into someone's life.

In one instance, I was serving as a short-term executive coach for a Native American woman who did not share my Christian perspective. The more I talked to her, the more I felt compelled to share a Bible passage with her out of either the book of Psalms or Proverbs, I no longer remember the exact passage. When this compulsion first popped up, I pushed it back down and said, "She is not interested in that, so why would I bring this up to her?" However, the urge to share the verse became so strong that I stopped what we were doing, explained myself, and asked for her permission to proceed and let her know that I was fine if she chose to decline. The woman granted permission and the verses spoke very directly and helpfully into her situation, and she was thankful I shared them with her.

When this divine guidance happens with another Christian person, I am not surprised because I believe the spirit of God is working through me to bring divine perspective to a fellow traveler on a similar path. In one such case, I was speaking with a client about his retirement plans. This was our first meeting and unbeknownst to me, he had prayed for divine guidance and direction. As I was speaking to him, a flood of revelation came to mind about him and his situation. When I finished speaking, he sat in stunned silence because the things I said answered his questions with divine guidance and counsel, and he knew I had no way of knowing his circumstances so intimately. I knew it wasn't me, but God speaking through me to this man's situation. At the end of that conversation, my client had clarity and knew what to do next.

These times of direct divine guidance are amazing and awe-inspiring. They are borne out of a deep and abiding rest in God's presence, which means spending daily time with Him. I am reminded of Brother Lawrence, a monk from many centuries ago who talked about practicing the presence of God in all we do, even if it's washing dishes in a commercial kitchen. We can be in communion or fellowship at any time.

"The fruit of the spirit is love, joy, peace, patience, kindness, goodness, faithfulness, gentleness, and self-control. Against such there is no law" (Galatians 5:22-23). These are virtues that I want to guide my every step and my every day, so I stay close to the source and supply of this fruit. I have experienced such a depth of hope and inspiration from my spiritual life. It is truly daily fuel for my journey.

In addition to spiritual learning for myself, as I said in Chapter 6, the best way to learn something is to teach it to others. I am part of the adult Sunday school teaching team at my church. My husband and I have been part of making this class a profound spiritual feast for adults. It takes hours of study and preparation to properly teach a Sunday school class, so we always learn the most when we teach. In addition to Sunday school, I also present at women's retreats, Women's Day celebrations, and other forums where a spiritual teacher is needed. My spiritual gifts include teaching, exhortation, and wisdom.

My life purpose is grounded in spiritual meaning, destiny, and calling. As a child, I was always wired to be a part of the helping profession. I saw psychology as a perfect fit with my spiritual beliefs and as a route to helping others in a deeper way. I didn't know until graduate school that most of psychology sees a fundamental disconnect between the profession and Christianity. A lot of psychology is rooted in humanism and a more decidedly atheistic perspective. I never knew or saw this, and I still see that the grander truths in life about man's search for meaning, purpose, and significance are rooted in spiritual realities, whether people call them that or not.

You may define spirituality in a way other than what I have described, and that is fine since each person chooses their own way. Spirituality is about that intangible nonmaterial reality of our lives. In organizations, it is the breath of life that inspires motivation, resolve, and commitment. There are reasons beyond the tangibles of money or other material objects that keep people working for you or you working for them. Knowing what inspires your life purpose helps you to live it more fully.

Identify and Set Your Compass

Spirituality is also a moral compass for life. There will be many opportunities to go left or right, and how you decide which way to go while staying grounded in your values is deeply spiritual. Life brings many decisions that will force you to consider your bottom lines, core values, and trade-offs. Some years ago, I faced such a dilemma. I had always said my priorities were God first, family second, and work third. During this season in my life, my husband was stationed far away from me and my mother was very ill in the last years of her life, also far away from me. The job I had at the time did not allow me the flexibility to freely and properly plan my schedule to see my husband and my mother once a month.

After some soul searching and difficult decision-making, I decided to leave my employer so that I could visit both of these people whom I cared about. After I made that decision, other opportunities opened up, including some with a prior employer. As a result, I suffered no monetary loss, gained lots of freedom, and saw my mother and husband in separate trips once a month. Consequently, when my mother later died, I had no regrets because I did what I thought was best. I participated in her care and I prioritized my relationship with her, even though the decision was difficult to make. It was like letting go of a trapeze in midair and grabbing for the next one, not knowing if it was going to be there or not. Sometimes, you just must take the leap.

As a leader you will make many tough decisions where the choices will seem daunting. What compass will you use to determine your values, priorities, and bottom lines? It's helpful to think about this in advance. Layoffs and downsizing are some of the most difficult business decisions leaders have to make. What will you do to bring dignity and respect to the process? How will you provide services for those who lose their jobs? What services will you provide? How will notifications be made? What severance packages will you offer? Will you do the layoff just before or after Christmas? Post a notice on the factory door with no one for people to talk to about the decision? How you handle all of these choices is a function of both your company culture and your personal values and bottom line. Who you are as a leader will show up in how the most difficult decisions are made and implemented.

Build Resilience

At other times, spiritual grounding is an important source of strength and resilience. In this life, not everyone is going to like you, appreciate you, or treat you well. Sometimes you will know why and other times you won't. When you are spiritually grounded, you can still choose to respond out of the values of your own character and to show up the way you want to regardless of what the other person is doing.

One day, I was doing a leadership training program at the Broadmoor Hotel, a five-star hotel and golf resort/spa in Colorado Springs. From minute one of the class, there was a White male participant in the class who went full-steam ahead to attack everything I said, to ask challenging questions in a disrespectful manner, and to cause chaos with his many interruptions. It was day one and things were not going well. It was clear both to me and the other participants that his questions were not designed to gather information, but rather to look for a way to throw me off and make me look bad. Although I had no problems answering his questions because I knew the material, that was not my concern.

The other members of the class were very uncomfortable, and no one knew why he was determined to attack me. I didn't know this man, had never met him before, and had not done anything to him. His responses were clearly over and above anything that was going on in the classroom, and I didn't know why. He purposefully competed with me though I was not competing with him. Finally, we came to a break and I asked to speak to him.

"I have noticed that you have been countering and disagreeing with everything I say, you are also using a clipped and loud tone of voice when you speak, and you constantly interrupt with questions that seem designed to trip me more than to get real answers. I am feeling disrespected and I also see that others are starting to shut down, talk less, look away, sigh when they hear your voice, and look tense. I am not sure what's happening; however, I wonder if we can take some time to talk about it?"

"You are right. I have been doing all those things and this is not my normal behavior. In fact, I am embarrassed because I don't really understand why I am doing this and I need to figure it out."

"Have I done something to offend you in any way?"

"Oh no, you haven't done anything at all. It's my problem. I just don't know what my problem is, and I need to think about it some more. Can we talk about it after lunch?"

"Yes, let's meet over lunch and then also take some additional time after we eat."

"In the meantime, I'll think about this some more," he said, "so we can talk about it. Also, I will stop my disruptive behavior immediately."

"OK. Thank you and I appreciate your commitment to an immediate change. I look forward to talking further at lunch."

The participant was fine the rest of the morning with no unusual comments, and then we met over lunch and continued our conversation after lunch while walking around the lake at the Broadmoor.

He said, "I don't know what the problem is, though initially I thought maybe it's because you are Black, but then so-and-so is also here this week and she too is a Black woman and I didn't have the same reaction to her. Anyway, I've thought about it some more and the difference is that you have a doctorate and so-and-so doesn't, so I was feeling competitive with you and as if I should also have my doctorate."

Having no idea of what to expect from this conversation, I was stunned. "Well OK, so what do you think this is about?"

"Well, obviously I feel as if I am behind and should be further along in my education too."

"Do you think you would have the same reaction if I too was a White male?"

He thought a moment, paused, and said, "Probably not. I know this sounds really bad; however, I am also trying to be honest with myself."

"So, as you hear yourself saying these things, what strikes you?"

We continued this conversation along these lines for a while until he came to some insights and epiphanies about his own preconceived notions, competitiveness, and ways of operating when he feels one-down. None of this was about me—it was about him—and so I had to stay calm and neutral enough to be the sounding board so he could hear himself, and to be the mirror so he could see himself. I was participating in his development. This was one of the most honest conversations of its type that I can remember. Most people who think these thoughts never verbalize them to someone like me. It took tremendous courage on his part to look at his behavior, which felt ego-dystonic from how he normally saw himself. In addition, it took a certain spiritual centeredness for me to hold the space for him to do this work.

The conversation also changed my life because it gave further proof to the idea that when "bad" things happen, it's not always about you, even if it seems to be. People have their own stuff that sometimes gets played out on you even though you are innocent. I know many people in my position who would not have tolerated the conversation and would have told him where to go; however, by hanging in there with him, we both got a gift and had a great rest of the week. After he worked this situation out in his mind and had a chance to process it, he was able to shift his behavior and show up differently for the rest of the seminar. What a relief—otherwise, it would have been a very long week.

At other times, things happen and we don't get to speak candidly with the people involved to see what's really going on, so we must get through those with our sense of self and character intact. In another situation, I signed up to attend an entrepreneurial seminar for business owners. I was looking forward to the meeting and had even signed up for a pre-meeting VIP day with a small group of other participants, as well as some other conference VIP events.

I showed up at the pre-meeting VIP event fully expecting to learn and enjoy participating. Right away I became the target of the leader of the seminar. At every turn, she viciously attacked for no reason that I could identify. Her behavior was so over the top that other participants got concerned and checked periodically to see how I was doing. I didn't know this woman and she didn't know me, so her immediate dislike had to be rooted in something beyond me. In this case, I never got to have any conversations to discover the problem, so I just concluded that maybe I reminded her of someone painful from her past.

This woman was fine when we were in the large group; however, whenever, we were in the small VIP session, she went on the rampage, and later in the week had convinced some other leaders from her organization to join in her attacks. As the week went on, it became increasingly difficult to motivate myself to leave the hotel room to attend the session. I had paid good money for this seminar and I wanted to finish the course, though it was very difficult. Every day when I woke up, I played a spiritual song—"Be Encouraged"—and sang it at least three times until my own spirit shifted into the place I needed to be to face the day.

I remember thinking about King David when he was running out of the palace to escape his son Absalom. Along the way, a man named Shimei from the house of Saul was cursing David and throwing stones at him. Abishai and the other men with David wanted to kill Shimei for cursing the King. II Samuel 1:10-12 records David's response: "...If he is cursing because the Lord said to him, 'Curse David,' who can ask, 'Why do you do this?'" David then said to Abishai and all his officials, "My son who is my own flesh, is trying to take my life. How much more then this Benjamite! Leave him alone; let him curse, for the Lord has told him to. It may be that the Lord will see my distress and repay me with good for the cursing I am receiving today."

David didn't just fight his own battles, even when he had the opportunity. On several occasions before he became King, David had the opportunity to kill King Saul, and though Saul was trying to kill David, David did not retaliate. David always saw God as the One who fought his battles, and frequently before battles with enemies, David would confer with God to ask, "Shall we go up?" If God said "No," then he didn't fight. For David, timing was everything. Though Shimei may have deserved to die, this was not the time.

Likewise, in my situation, I tried to discern the spiritual message of all these events. I saw it as a warning not to get involved with this organization. Though others could continue with it, I was to come out from among them. I paid attention to the spiritual warning and chose not to remain a part of that community and not to fight back.

Later that week, at the end of the seminar, several people came up to me and remarked about how I handled myself while unfairly under fire. They couldn't explain what happened, but said they didn't know if they could maintain such composure and grace under fire. God gave me everything I needed to show up wearing His fruit of the Spirit despite the unfair insults hurled at me. Spiritual resilience is something I need every day.

What fuels your resilience so that you present yourself in a positive light even if others do not? What strategies do you have in place to keep calm when others are losing their heads around you? As the senior leader, your emotional responses will reverberate throughout the organization. If you yell and scream, curse, or rake others over the coals, it sets a tone for the whole organization. Your subordinate leaders will feel comfortable in using the same approaches with their people and teams. Your behavior more than your words determines the organizational culture you create. Your own spiritual grounding and resilience will enable you to remain calm under fire and decent even when others are not. Leadership is about being proactive and responsive rather than reactive. Those who lead take time to do what is best even if it's not easy.

One of my clients reported to the top leader in his organization. The top boss was a volatile, screaming type of boss. My client had the disposition of a calm peacemaker, so his office became the first aid station for battered employees. Discouraged employees streamed in to get bandaged after their beatings from the top leader. Think of how much time and productivity was lost as a result of the senior leader's style and approach. Part of our work together included showing the senior leader the cost of his

behavior and the opportunity for having a more positive business impact with other approaches. My client had to get comfortable providing difficult feedback to a difficult boss.

Lessons Learned

1. Develop character and a moral compass. Get grounded in your values.
2. Decide what's important to you. Identify bottom lines and trade-offs.
3. Practice resilience. Tap into the source of love, hope, inspiration, faith, peace, and forgiveness.

Questions to Ask Yourself

1. How do I stay centered and grounded in who I want to be every day?
2. What strength do I access to love the unlovable and to forgive the unforgivable?
3. How do I need to further build my spiritual strength?

Chapter Eight

Practice Gratitude

"A Thankful Heart Opens the Doors of Abundance"

Every Day is Thanksgiving

"Thanks": such a beautiful and important word for our social and business interactions. Even when I only knew three German phrases, *danke schön* was one of them. Thanksgiving is a posture of the heart that keeps me positive and appreciative about what is present in my life. I recognize daily that I am richly blessed in so many ways.

Thanks to God

Each day I wake up, I am thankful to God for another day of life. I am thankful for a sound body and mind. I am thankful for food, shelter, and clothing. I am thankful for a loving husband, father, brothers, sister, and other family and friends. I am thankful for financial prosperity and for every opportunity to learn and serve. I could fill an entire book with all the blessings for which I am thankful.

Thanks to my Mother and Father

I am thankful for all the deposits my parents made into my life and all that I learned or inherited from them. My intelligence first belonged to them; they shared it with me.

I am thankful to my mother for the creativity I received, her entrepreneurial risk-taking spirit, her gift of conversation and public speaking, her generosity, and her gratitude.

I am thankful to my father for always believing in me and my dreams, for perseverance, hard-work, dedication, persistence, stability, financial sensibility, and steadfast love.

Maternal Grandmother Carrin

From my grandmother, I am thankful for a love of all people and a valuing of travel and diverse cultures. I also thank my grandmother for her gift of hospitality.

Paternal Grandmother Rosa

Born in the 1800s, her life was anything but easy. I thank Grandmother Rosa for her enduring love and faith. She and her children lived on her daily prayers, and no matter the hardships, she continued to love them and to expect the best of character from them. She was a true pioneer woman.

Great Aunt Jean

From my great aunt, I learned to be both an aunt and a great aunt. She exposed me to the world through unique cards and gifts, and demonstrated the value of being a creative free spirit.

Godmother Aunt Julia

From my Aunt Julia, I learned the eternal and everlasting nature of unconditional love, which nothing stops.

    I recently held a friend and family Thanksgiving party for those who were special and meaningful to my life in my formative years. Many peers and seniors are now starting to transition to the next life, and I wanted to let those who remain know how important they are to me even though I am no longer in Baltimore and have been gone for many years. I shared reflections about each person in attendance and thanked them for their place in my life. Each person also received thank-you gifts. I didn't want another person to leave the planet without my expressing thanks and gratitude to them. About twenty-five people attended, their ages ranging from fifty years to more than ninety.

    At work, I regularly employ subcontractors and others to provide services to clients of my company,

TRANSLEADERSHIP, INC. When I write their checks, I also send a personal note of thanks on my informal TRANSLEADERSHIP, INC. stationery. I take the time to acknowledge each person's specific contributions to our success. This act alone keeps thankfulness in my heart. It's nearly impossible to be negative and bitter while also being thankful. Thankfulness and gratitude are medicine for the soul. And people have reported having enjoyed receiving these notes.

When I was at the Center for Creative Leadership (CCL), they had a tradition of sending Valentine's cards, which I absolutely loved, and sometimes I still send them. Spreading love to others was something that resonated with me. Christmas is a busy time for me and my family, so I rarely get to send many if any Christmas cards; I'm more likely to send New Year's cards. In recent years, I have discovered Thanksgiving cards, and this has been very exciting because I am now adopting this holiday as my time to thank and appreciate my business associates and clients.

My mother died exactly one week before Thanksgiving. For many people, these kinds of anniversary dates can be traumatic; however, I thought it only fitting that she should leave at Thanksgiving because gratitude and thankfulness were two of her most powerful legacies to us. Consequently, Thanksgiving is now an occasion to remember her life of thankfulness and to continue to pass the gift forward to others. I have seen how a thankful heart opens the doors of abundance.

The Power of Celebration

Closely associated with gratitude is the concept of celebration. Societies have celebrations like weddings, coming of age parties, birthdays, and other events to mark important occasions and milestones. When I left my private practice at Air Regional Hospital at Maxwell Air Force Base in Montgomery, Alabama, I had at least thirty children in my care. I had come to love them, and they me. Most were very sad that I was leaving, so I decided to do something unprecedented, which was to have a special costume celebration party for all of them. Letters went out to parents explaining the invitation to the party and letting them know that if they chose to attend the children might see others they knew from the community. Typically, such matters are highly confidential, and no one knows who is coming to the clinic.

As it turns out, almost all the children chose to attend the party, which was held in our clinic's recreation room. Several work colleagues served as chaperones. The children showed up in their Ninja Turtle and other superhero costumes. We played games, ate food, popped lots of balloons, and generally had an exciting time. One little boy was shocked to see so many other children; he later told me that the number of children who came was a testimony to the relationship I had with them and the impact of that relationship. He was very pleased to see this result.

If private practices can have celebration parties, then certainly other workplaces can too. In my consulting work, I have found that many organizations are running so fast and furiously that they don't take the time to say "thank you" or to celebrate except for in the most cursory ways. When people give so much of themselves to create a successful result for the business, then these contributions need to be acknowledged in ways that are meaningful to the employees and commensurate with the prosperity they have brought. A celebration can be as simple or elaborate as practicable, from donuts or pizza in the office to happy hour at a local favorite spot, a banquet dinner at a local venue, a mountain ski trip with spouses and partners invited, or even family trips to Hawaii.

Organizations with the most cohesive work teams who gladly produce are usually the ones who celebrate even if it seems they don't have time. Taking the time communicates your valuing of your workforce and your acknowledgement of their sacrifices.

Lessons Learned

1. A heartfelt thank you in the language of the person being thanked is often more valuable than money.
2. Thanksgiving and gratitude keep the heart open and positive.
3. Celebrating those who make success possible is the greatest investment you can make.

Questions to Ask Yourself

1. How do I now say thank you to the people who make our success possible?
2. What celebrations do we now have and what more may be valuable to show appreciation?
3. To what extent do my people know how much they mean to me?

Celebrate yourself by taking your leadership development to the next level.

Request a complimentary consultation call with me by going to:

http://transleadership.com/services/consultation-request/

Chapter Nine

Encourage and Build Others

"Leaders Are Builders of People and Dreams"

Leaders are first responsible for building and developing themselves—if they skip this step, they will not be equipped to build others. Secondly, leaders build and develop other talented individuals. Thirdly, leaders build high-performance teams, and then leaders build organizations that consist of multiple high-performance teams staffed by talented and prepared individuals.

Many of my clients are scientists, engineers, or others with technical skills, though they struggle with the leadership piece. They have risen in the ranks because of their expertise and don't yet know the best ways to get the most out of others. Much of my work is focused on helping them to develop talented individuals, high-performance teams, and nimble learning organizations that innovate, take advantage of market opportunities, and gain a competitive edge by adding more value.

Although the business goals and results are important—crucial—it's been my experience that these don't happen without leadership, which includes attention to relationships, learning, and development. In addition to building their own people, teams, and organizations, effective leaders also learn to collaborate with both internal and external partners. Many know how to compete or how to advocate; fewer know how to collaborate. Ultimately, great leaders are builders of people and dreams.

I provide my clients with a safe and confidential platform for envisioning the future, developing skills, and building the organizations they most want to lead. They too must grow to become leaders for the organizations they envision. I have seen some situations where the organization has outpaced the leader in the self-development process. Such organizations often feel stymied and held back because their bosses do not yet possess the skills to support them. My preference is to prepare the leaders first whenever possible.

One of my clients was in a situation where his company's opportunities were coming at such an accelerated rate that they had already outgrown their infrastructure. We had to quickly shore up the foundation and build more infrastructure to accommodate the larger business he was building. He had very good people who were so taxed with the workload that they had no time for training or learning, both of which were necessary with the new opportunities. In this context, mistakes increased, and unnecessary expenses and financial losses due to preventable errors and rework were causing a reduction in profitability that if continued could also have cost the company its excellent reputation.

In another case, a client who had spent more than twenty-five years in operations in a manufacturing environment had to learn to better influence key stakeholders. He was getting nowhere pushing his agenda or advocating for his solutions. He had to learn to listen more deeply to others and their concerns, to understand their challenges, and then to speak their language and cocreate win-win solutions with them. Prior to learning those skills, he was hitting his head against the proverbial brick wall.

Another more innovative and visionary client tended to see what others didn't see on the horizon, but because they couldn't see it, his approach was not an easy sell. Although a senior leader himself, the other stakeholders were more senior than he, and he did not have the firepower to outgun them. When he went head-to-head with them from a power position, they ganged up on him and he lost. He had to learn to work behind the scenes through some of his junior personnel to demonstrate the value of an approach and then to present the results in a matter-of-fact, scientific, and dispassionate manner without disparaging anyone. After figuring this out, he gained key allies among those who previously had fought him, and they were able to successfully move forward together.

A client in China was leading a geographically dispersed global team. Each stakeholder had hidden agendas about what was most important to them, and those hidden agendas prevented the team from adopting a mutually agreeable, enterprise-wide agenda for the company. Until these issues were identified and addressed, her team was stuck.

In another case, a client was in a fast-moving global company where the European bosses were making strategic acquisitions and making decisions (with limited information) about which businesses should be continued and which should be deleted. Some decisions were made about my client's line of business that did not fit the facts of the situation. He had to assemble facts, get an audience with the big bosses, make a presentation, and offer financially profitable alternatives—which he did successfully, thus saving his business unit to continue to add value to the company.

In all of these and other client situations, I have used an approach that can be described as follows:

THE TRANSLEADERSHIP, INC. APPROACH

1. Identify the key question or challenge.
2. Listen deeply for opportunities the client may not have identified.
3. Name signature strengths of the client and company.
4. Identify areas for new learning.
5. Consider and create strategies for influencing key stakeholders.
6. Prepare workable scenarios.
7. Practice implementing the scenarios.
8. Test the plan in real life.
9. Review the results.
10. Tweak the plan and continue until results are achieved.

I love this work and know that I am helping to build and develop those who build and develop others. It's very rewarding to see the turnarounds that clients make in their direction, approaches, and results.

Lessons Learned

1. Develop yourself and be a role model.
2. Build and serve other individual leaders.
3. Build and develop both teams and organizations.

Questions to Ask Yourself

1. What development do my people most need right now?
2. What development do I most need to best develop my people?
3. How can TRANSLEADERSHIP, INC. potentially help me?

Chapter Ten

Play Your Music

"You Are the Instrument of Your Leadership"

Each of you has been specially gifted with talents and abilities unique to you in their combination. This unique combination allows you to play your special music that will resonate with those who are supposed to hear and follow you. Sometimes you will know they are watching and following, sometimes you will find out later, and at other times you may never know. Each instrument has a purpose and a special sound. The trumpet is not the flute and the piano is not the drum. Each instrument has its own place and purpose in the song to be played. The point is to play your song. Music is powerful in its ability to move and touch us emotionally at our deepest core. Music engages all parts of us and is memorable even when little else may be.

Sometime after I graduated with my PhD, my grandmother gave a celebration party at her house. Relatives attended from New York, Philadelphia, Baltimore, and Virginia. Years later, one of my cousins from Baltimore entered the Navy under a health professions scholarship and became a physician. During the years of my mother's illness, I occasionally saw this cousin in the local hospitals where she was an intern and a resident. Following her academic preparation, she served as a Navy officer and MD. One day, she decided to tell me the story of how she chose to pursue her career path. At the party my grandmother gave for my PhD, she looked at me and said, "This person is in my family. She is my cousin, and if she can do this, then so can I." She filed that away and pursued her vision. I never knew this until years later when she shared it. She heard the music and it resonated with her. You never know who is listening or watching.

Some years ago, a consulting psychologist colleague and I conducted a senior consultant workshop for our peers at the annual Midwinter Conference (MWC) of the Society for

Consulting Psychologists. Our intention was to provide a place for our colleagues to share more deeply and to talk about the legacy they wanted to leave. The workshop included lots of prework to include bringing a memorable song to share with the group. In the spirit of role modeling, my colleague and I also shared our stories and songs. My colleague selected a song I did not know, "Put Your Records On" by British artist Corinne Bailey Rae. A small portion of the lyrics say, "I hope you get your dreams. Just go ahead let your hair down. You're going to find yourself somewhere, somehow."

I like a smattering of all styles of music, though my personal favorite is gospel. Occasionally a song comes to me and I am inspired to sing it; thankfully, the minister of music at my church is a flexible woman of God who helps me learn to sing the song that speaks powerfully to me in that season. As I have no musical training, this is truly a labor of love on her part. Your voice has its own music and your people are listening for your voice in the marketplace.

Even the Bible talks about the value of speaking intelligible words in public assembly. Following the music analogy, I Corinthians 14: 7-9 says, "Even in the case of lifeless things that make sounds, such as the flute or harp, how will anyone know what tune is being played unless there is a distinction in the notes? Again, if the trumpet does not sound a clear call, who will get ready for battle? So it is with you. Unless you speak intelligible words with your tongue, how will anyone know what you are saying? You will just be speaking into the air."

The words you speak are for the purpose of fulfilling your primary purpose and mission as a leader. This is the list we use in thinking about the core responsibilities of leaders.

The Key Tasks and Responsibilities of Senior Leaders

1. Set Vision and Direction
2. Create and Maintain an Effective Organizational Culture

3. Provide Resources for Success
4. Develop Key Leaders Who Develop Other Leaders and Teams
5. Celebrate and Reward Success
6. Identify Opportunities to Add Value and Get Results
7. Determine and Take the Next Best Step

Check to see how your actions line up with these responsibilities and where there is room for continued growth and development.

Lessons Learned

1. Leaders Make a Difference—Play Your Music
2. Inspire and Call Others with Your Unique Song
3. You Are the Instrument of Your Leadership

Questions to Ask Yourself

1. What symphonies, jazz tunes, gospel, country, rock, or other compositions am I destined to play?
2. Who is listening and who is waiting for me to create what only I can?
3. What message do I want to deliver? Whom do I want to inspire?

**You are the instrument of your leadership.
Play your music.**

Learn more about how TRANSLEADERSHIP, INC. and Dr. Karen can show you how to deliver more dynamic organizational results:

1. Visit our website at www.transleadership.com
2. Take the Lead Yourself First Leadership Assessment:
3. http://transleadership.com/resources/development1-assessment/
4. Watch Dr. Karen's video on The Top Ten Tips for Leading High-Performance Teams:
5. http://transleadership.com/resources/team-video1/
6. Book Dr. Karen for speaking engagements:
7. http://transleadership.com/services/speaking-form/
8. Request a complimentary consultation with Dr. Karen:
9. http://transleadership.com/services/consultation-request/
10. Purchase another copy of this book for a friend:
11. http://transleadership.com/resources/book-lead-yourself-first/

Summary of Lessons Learned

1. Set a clear compelling vision and intention for your life.
2. Have faith that somehow, some way, the vision will come to fruition if you continue to pursue it.
3. Knock until the door—or another door—opens.
4. Run your own race.
5. Focus on your own destination/finish line.
6. Know your strengths and development needs and create your strategies for your best success.
7. Access and add to your network on a regular basis.
8. Look for opportunities in the far-reaching corners of your current experiences.
9. See each experience and opportunity as a learning tool to prepare you for even greater future opportunities.
10. Encourage and reinforce what you want, and you will get more of it.
11. Use strengths as your foundation for success. Identify and build on "what's right" with this picture.
12. See mistakes as positive learning opportunities.
13. Face your fears and do it anyway.
14. Surround yourself with people who challenge you, won't let you give up, and who also support you.
15. Practice and repeat an action until the fear goes away and you develop the skill.

16. Invest in yourself first and then also in your people and your organization.
17. Prioritize all kinds of continuous learning such as conferences, books, webinars/recordings, seminars, and training programs.
18. Learn from all kinds of people, be they from the past or present. Those from the past are still living through the legacy of their recorded experiences.
19. Develop character and a moral compass. Get grounded in your values.
20. Decide what's important to you. Identify bottom lines and trade-offs.
21. Practice resilience. Tap into the source of love, hope, inspiration, faith, peace, and forgiveness.
22. A heartfelt thank you in the language of the person being thanked is often more valuable than money.
23. Thanksgiving and gratitude keep the heart open and positive.
24. Celebrating those who make success possible is the greatest investment you can make.
25. Develop yourself and be a role model.
26. Build and serve other individual leaders.
27. Build and develop both teams and organizations.
28. Leaders make a difference—play your music.
29. Inspire and call others with your unique song.
30. You are the instrument of your leadership.

Summary of Questions to Ask Yourself

1. What is the compelling vision I hold for myself? For my organization? What do I want to see in the future?
2. How can I encourage myself in pursuing this vision even when what I see in the present seems far from that future picture?
3. What qualities/skills do I already have to realize this vision? What else will I need to learn?
4. When have I had to run my own race in a way that differed from others? What did I learn?
5. When have I mistakenly gone the way of the masses when my own journey was unique? What were the prices/consequences to be paid?
6. What's happening right now for me personally or the organization I lead that requires a unique race? What might I need to implement, and how will I stay focused?
7. What blizzard food have I found in my life? What gourmet food was I able to create with the blizzard food?
8. What career pieces have I been able to put together from unexpected opportunities or options I created for myself?
9. How can I show others how to access these same resources in their own lives?
10. What punishment do I need to stop before I can care for my team more perfectly?

11. What additional opportunities for positive reinforcement can I identify in my workplace? What will this encouragement look like day-to-day?
12. How can I encourage and support myself to be a better leader?
13. What have I learned from persisting through fears that I can share with someone else?
14. In what ways has my confidence and skill level been expanded by the challenges I have faced and overcome?
15. What am I now avoiding that I just need to do? Whom can I enlist as my sergeant and belay master?
16. From what resources am I currently learning? What am I learning from these resources?
17. What else do I need to learn, and where can I go for this learning?
18. How am I creating a continuous learning organization in my workplace? What more can I do to seed and water learning in my organization?
19. How do I stay centered and grounded in who I want to be every day?
20. What strength do I access to love the unlovable and to forgive the unforgivable?
21. How do I need to further build my spiritual strength?
22. How do I now say thank you to the people who make our success possible?
23. What celebrations do we now have and what more may be valuable to show appreciation?
24. To what extent do my people know how much they mean to me?
25. What development do my people most need right now?

26. What development do I most need to best develop my people?
27. How can TRANSLEADERSHIP, INC. potentially help me?
28. What symphonies, jazz tunes, gospel, country, rock, or other compositions am I destined to play?
29. Who is listening and who is waiting for me to create what only I can?
30. What message do I want to deliver? Who do I want to inspire?

Epilogue

Where I Am From

Born the oldest of four children to Morris and Yvonne Wilson in the Chesapeake Bay harbor town of Baltimore, Maryland, my parents say I was born talking, leading, creating stories, and later showing my next oldest brother how to escape from the crib. Back then, children could take the bus downtown without fear of being harmed. Winos at the docks and piers tipped their hats or bottles and said "good morning" as the seagulls squawked above.

The smell of Old Bay seasoning in delectable, mouth-watering, exquisite Maryland crab cakes wafted on the air to the sounds of waitresses saying, "Hon, what can I get you?" Ethnic neighborhoods and endless row houses formed a checkerboard of culinary and cultural delights such as Chinatown and Little Italy. Baltimore was the home of the Orioles, the Colts, and the Bullets, and sports heroes like Jim Palmer, Jim Parker, and Johnny Unitas.

Parents picketed outside of my school, not wanting Black children to attend even as my Jewish friend Emily and I stood on the playground missing soccer balls together and dreaming of visits to each other's homes only to later learn this could never happen. No real work ever happened on Jewish holidays, when most of the teachers and students were gone. At school, we acknowledged Christmas and Easter and learned about Hanukkah, dreidels, Passover, and Matzo.

Summers were spent on the Atlantic Ocean at local beaches like Fort Smallwood, or out of town in Wildwood, New Jersey or on the Boardwalk in Atlantic City, long before the casinos. Saltwater taffy, cotton candy, and seashells were the welcome treasures of a summer well spent. Other summers were spent in Harlem taking the subway, swimming at the neighborhood pool, attending summer school, and speaking English to children speaking Spanish on the playground while we all played together and my cousins translated.

I grew up in a conservative church where musical instruments were not permitted even for weddings, where only men were leaders, and women and girls always wore skirts. We attended church for most of the day on Sunday into the night, and on Wednesday night. It was at church that I learned to study, teach, and deliver public speeches.

As a skirted pioneer Girl Scout, I roasted marshmallows in the fire, cooked Girl Scout stew, and dug fire pits and latrines. Marching in parades, I proudly displayed badges up the front and down the back of my sash.

Although my grandmother—my mother's mother—only lived across town, spending the night at her house was like being in another world, filled with the noises and sounds of the city. Waking up to the familiar and rhythmic sound of the streetcars on the tracks and watching the sparks of the overhead wires were pure delight and excitement compared to our quiet neighborhood without public transportation. With the streetcar, you never needed an alarm clock. It was both an exciting and comforting sound, because it meant Grandmother was with us.

Grandmother was the consummate host and a cook par excellence. No one was ever a stranger in her home. Every friend was warmly welcomed and integrated into the family as if a long-lost relative. People traveled far and wide to indulge in her signature sweet potato pie, fried oysters, and fresh steamed crabs by the bushel.

My brother Morris and I were her overnight helpers the day before Thanksgiving. We picked greens, shelled shrimp, and set the table with the fine china. On Thanksgiving Day, Grandmother never had less than thirty guests at her dining room table, and at the children's table she always served cran-apple juice—in wine glasses, so we would feel special. Pa, my grandfather, always went hunting for Thanksgiving, and so in addition to the traditional turkey, the table was always set with whatever wild game he'd caught that year—anything from deer to rabbit, squirrel, duck, or opossum. In a moment of mischief, Pa would always remove the heavy flatiron off the bushel crab barrel to let one escape; Grandmother would then chase him and the crab with a giant set of tongs. We children loved this annual game of "cat and crab."

Christmas was my mother's favorite holiday. The festivities began promptly at midnight with my father waking us up to open all the gifts at our home, and then we'd pile into the car and head to Grandmother's house to open gifts. We continued house to house till morning, when we'd take a nap and later head to the home of friends for an early dinner.

By profession, my mother was a nurse; however, over the years she also was a pioneer woman and did many nontraditional jobs, including driving a mail truck in a time when women didn't do such things. Some years ago, she left this world way too early, her vibrant and vivacious light extinguished by many of the same illnesses that threaten me—though with Olympic torch in hand, I constantly outrun them both for me and for her. She died a week before Thanksgiving, which annually reminds me of all I have to be thankful and grateful for.

My father is from Blackstone, Virginia. He is the youngest child of my grandmother Rosa, who struggled in deep poverty against all odds to raise seven children while living on a slave plantation. Their house was not a real house as you and I would count houses—it was later used as a chicken coop. Though not much of a house, theirs was a home full of love and sacrifice, with my grandmother Rosa not always knowing how she would feed her children though committed to do so. Endlessly resourceful and an excellent cook—that was still her job for the former slave owners—she prayed to God, made flour stretch, and fed her children sometimes catching fish using a makeshift pole and line. She could always make something out of nothing. Born in the 1800s to parents whose parents had been slaves on the plantation, she was part of my life until 1978.

Daddy was the only child to finish high school. After moving to Baltimore, he eventually became a bus driver and later finished college and ended his career as a research and planning executive for the Mass Transit Administration. He regularly speaks of the hand of God in his life leading and guiding him even when he didn't know it. He remembers his mother's daily prayers for each of her children and knows he was the recipient of their blessing.

So, where am I from? I was named Karen Yvette after my grandmother Carrin and my mother Yvonne. My father's name, Wilson, reminds me that I am part of the sons and daughters of those who, through great will and determination, under the hand of God, triumphed over daunting odds. Deeply rooted in African-American soil with a strain of Cherokee from my maternal great-grandfather, I come from people who have known adversity, perseverance, and success. I am from those Africans who entered slave ships on the Atlantic side of Africa, passing through the doors of no return, and who made it through the middle passage, slavery, and other trials so that I can stand before you today. I am from a mighty lineage of those who know that our strength and power extend beyond the physical to the spiritual; I am from the place where I will ultimately return, the Ancient of Days.

Personal Aspirational Vision Statement

I radiate the illuminating light of God's wisdom and discernment. My life is meaningful, and I am full of purpose, passion, and energy. My life is powered by divine love. I love my family, friends, and others with the fullness of the love I have received. My life is a gift to be opened, explored, and shared. As an eternal flower always growing and blossoming, I walk in the aloha spirit of welcome and akwaaba. Love, joy, peace, and abundance are my daily companions. I inspire myself and others to the full greatness to which we have been called.

My family thrives and has enough of everything for a joyous and fulfilled life. We have a wealth of time, freedom, and abundant financial resources to fund all our desired activities. Our home is a haven of rest, relaxation, peace, and eclectic beauty. We are hospitable and enjoy sharing our bounty with others. My husband and I delight in each other and feel blessed to spend our years together. Our nieces, great-nieces and great-nephews, and godchildren are loved and nurtured in our care where they may find comfort, direction, encouragement, and support for their dreams. Our days are exciting with many divine appointments.

At work, we create products, processes, and experiences that transform lives. Because of our work, people live more fulfilled lives, respond powerfully to their callings, live out their destinies, and realize their dreams. Our clients and associates significantly impact and enable effective leadership and purposeful living. Every day is filled with learning, growth, discovery, and possibility. We work positively, creatively, and collaboratively, living the best of all we believe. Choices and options are bountiful and limitations few. In all circumstances, I walk daily in thanksgiving and gratitude.

Dr. Karen Y. Wilson-Starks

President and CEO

TRANSLEADERSHIP, INC.

www.ingramcontent.com/pod-product-compliance
Lightning Source LLC
Chambersburg PA
CBHW071526080526
44588CB00011B/1574